Business Result

SECOND EDITION

Intermediate *Teacher's Book*

John Hughes
& Lynne White

OXFORD
UNIVERSITY PRESS

Great Clarendon Street, Oxford, OX2 6DP, United Kingdom

Oxford University Press is a department of the University of Oxford.
It furthers the University's objective of excellence in research, scholarship,
and education by publishing worldwide. Oxford is a registered trade
mark of Oxford University Press in the UK and in certain other countries

ISBN: 978 0 19 473892 7   Book
ISBN: 978 0 19 473891 0   Pack

Printed in China

This book is printed on paper from certified and well-managed sources

ACKNOWLEDGEMENTS

Cover image: Getty Images/Gary Burchell

Back cover photograph: Oxford University Press building/David Fisher

Contents

Introduction

The course

Who is *Business Result Second Edition* for?

Business Result Second Edition is a comprehensive multi-level course in business English suitable for a wide range of learners. The main emphasis is on *enabling* your students; helping them to communicate more effectively in their working lives.

In-work students

Unlike many business English courses, *Business Result Second Edition* addresses the language and communication needs of employees at all levels of an organization, who need to use English at work. It recognizes that the business world is truly international and that many people working in a modern, global environment spend much of their time doing everyday tasks in English – communicating with colleagues and work contacts by phone, via email and in a range of face-to-face situations, such as formal and informal meetings/discussions, and various planned and unplanned social encounters. It contains topics and activities that allow the students to participate in a way that is relevant to them, whatever their level in their company or organization.

Pre-work learners

Business Result Second Edition can also be used with pre-work learners at college level. The course covers a variety of engaging topics over the 15 units, so students without much work experience will receive a wide-ranging overview of the business world, as well as acquiring the key communication skills they will need in their future working lives. Each unit in this *Teacher's Book* contains suggestions for adapting the material to the needs of these students.

One-to-one teaching

Many of the activities in the book are designed for use with groups of students, but they can also be easily adapted to suit a one-to-one teaching situation. Notes in the individual *Teacher's Book* units offer suggestions and help with this.

What approach does *Business Result Second Edition* take?

Business Result Second Edition helps students communicate in English in real-life work situations. The priority at all times is on enabling them to do so more effectively and with confidence. The target language in each unit has been carefully selected to ensure that students will be equipped with genuinely useful, transferable language that they can take out of the classroom and use immediately in the workplace.

The course recognizes that, with so many businesses now being staffed by people of different nationalities, there is an increasing trend towards using English as the language of internal communication in many organizations. As well as learning appropriate language for communicating externally – with clients or suppliers, for example – students are also given the opportunity to practise in situations that take place within an organization, such as giving a report, making arrangements and taking part in meetings.

The main emphasis of the course is on the students speaking and trying out the target language in meaningful and authentic ways; it is expected that a large proportion of the lesson time will be spent on activating students' interest and encouraging them to talk. The material intentionally takes a communicative, heads-up approach, maximizing the amount of classroom time available to focus on and practise the target language. However, you will also find that there is plenty of support in terms of reference notes, written practice and review material.

The syllabus is essentially communication-driven. The topics in each of the 15 units have been chosen because of their relevance to modern business and the world of work. Vocabulary is presented in realistic contexts with reference to real companies or organizations. Grammar is also a key element of each unit. It is presented in an authentic context and ensures that students pay attention to accuracy, as well as become more proficient at expressing themselves clearly and precisely. The *Business communication* sections ensure that students are provided with a range of key expressions they can use immediately, both in the classroom and in their day-to-day work.

STUDENT'S BOOK

The *Student's Book* pack

The *Student's Book* pack offers a blend of classroom teaching and self-study, with an emphasis on flexibility and time-efficiency. Each of the 15 *Student's Book* units provides around four hours of classroom material with the potential for two to three hours of additional study using other materials in the pack.

The materials that support the *Student's Book* units are:
- *Viewpoint* video lessons
- Practice files
- Progress tests
- Photocopiable worksheets
- *Online practice*

More information on all of these materials and how to use them can be found later in these Introduction pages.

Key features of a unit

Starting point

Each unit opens with some lead-in questions to raise awareness of, and interest in, the unit theme. Use these questions to help you establish what students already know about the topic and how it relates to their own working lives. These questions can usually be discussed as a class or in small groups.

Working with words

This first main section introduces key vocabulary in a variety of ways, including authentic reading texts, listening texts and visuals. Students are also encouraged to look at how different forms of words (verbs, adjectives and nouns) can be built from the same root, or to look at common combinations (e.g. verb + noun, adjective + noun) that will help them to expand their personal lexicon more rapidly. This section also offers opportunities to work on your students' reading and listening skills.

Language at work

The grammar is looked at from a communicative point of view; this will meet your students' expectations with regard to learning form and meaning, but also reminds them how the grammar they need to learn commonly occurs in business and work situations. The *Language point* highlights the target grammar structures, which are then practised in authentic work contexts.

Practically speaking

This section looks at various practical aspects of everyday communication and social interaction from a 'how to' perspective – for example, *How to show interest, How to address people* – as well as useful ways that we use language in communication, such as *say* and *tell*.

Business communication

This section focuses on one of five broad communication themes – meetings, presenting, exchanging information, phone calls and socializing. These are treated differently throughout the book so that, for example, students are able to practise exchanging information on the phone as well as face-to-face, or compare the different language needed for giving formal and informal presentations. Typically, the section begins with students listening to an example situation (a meeting, a presentation, a social encounter, a series of phone calls). They focus on *Key expressions* used by the speakers which are listed on the page. They are then given the opportunity to practise these in various controlled and more open work-related tasks.

Tips

Throughout each unit, there are short, practical tips with useful language points arising from a particular section or exercise.

Talking point

All units end with a *Talking point*. These provide the opportunity for students to discuss a range of business concepts, approaches and ideas and how they might apply these in their own work. All of the topics relate to the unit theme and provide the opportunity for students to use the language from the unit.

The *Talking point* follows a three-part structure: Input (a short text, listening or infographic), Discussion, Task.

*Note that in two units (units 2 and 11) the *Talking point* format is presented as a game. This is designed to be fun and is aimed at recycling the language from the unit.

Viewpoint

After every three units there is a two-page *Viewpoint* video lesson. The topic of the *Viewpoint* lesson relates to a theme from the preceding units and includes interviews with expert speakers and case studies of real companies. Each *Viewpoint* has a number of short videos and is divided

into three or four sections. Each lesson usually opens with an introduction to the topic and interviews with people discussing the topic. Key words and phrases are then introduced before students watch the main video section. Here, students can develop listening and note-taking skills with language presented in an authentic context. Each lesson ends with activities to give students speaking practice discussing the topic of the lesson.

Additional material

At the back of the *Student's Book*, you will find the following sections.

Practice files

These provide unit-by-unit support for your classroom work. Each file provides additional practice of target language from the three main unit sections, *Working with words*, *Language at work* and *Business communication* and can be used in two ways:

For extra practice in class – refer students to this section for more controlled practice of new vocabulary, grammar or key expressions before moving to the next stage. The optimum point at which to do this is indicated by cross-references in the *Student's Book* unit and the teaching notes in this book.

For self-study – students can complete and self-check the exercises for review and revision outside class.

Answers for the *Practice file* exercises appear on pages 93–96 of this book.

Communication activities

Additional information for pairwork and group activities.

Audio scripts

Irregular verb list

TEACHER'S BOOK

What's in each unit?

Unit content

This provides an overview of the main aims and objectives of the unit.

Context

This section not only provides information on the teaching points covered in the unit, but also offers some background information on the main business theme of the unit and its importance in the current business world. If you are less familiar with the world of business, you will find this section especially helpful to read before starting a unit.

Teaching notes and answers

Notes on managing the *Student's Book* exercises and various activities are given throughout, with suggested variations that you might like to try. You will find comprehensive answers to all *Student's Book* exercises, as well as notes on possible responses to discussion questions.

One-to-one

In general, you will find that *Business Result Second Edition* can be used with any size of class. However, with one-to-one students you will find that activities which have been designed with groups of students in mind will need some adaptation. The *Teacher's Book* provides suggestions for how to adapt group work activities successfully for one-to-one classes.

Pre-work learners

Although most users of *Business Result Second Edition* will be students who are already in work, you may also be teaching classes of students who have little or no experience of the business world. The *Teacher's Book* provides suggestions for how to adapt certain questions or tasks in the book to their needs, and extra notes are given for these types of learners.

Extension

With some students it may be appropriate to extend an exercise in some way or relate the language point more specifically to a particular group of students. Suggestions on how to do this are given where appropriate.

Extra activity

If you have time or would like to develop further areas of language competence, extra activities are suggested where they naturally follow the order of activities in the *Student's Book*. For example, if your students need writing practice or need to build more confidence with speaking, extra follow-up ideas may be provided.

Alternative

With some students it may be preferable to approach an activity in a different way, depending on their level or their interests. These options are provided where appropriate.

Pronunciation

Tips on teaching pronunciation and helping students improve their intelligibility are provided where there is a logical need for them. These often appear where new vocabulary is taught, or for making key expressions sound more natural and fluent.

Dictionary skills

It's helpful to encourage students to use a good dictionary in class and the relevant notes suggest moments in the lesson when it may be useful to develop your students' skills in using dictionaries.

USING THE COURSE

How to use *Business Result Second Edition* to fit your teaching context

Business Result Second Edition provides all the flexibility you need as a teacher. The syllabus and content has been carefully designed so that it can be used either from start to finish or in a modular way, allowing you to tailor the course to suit your and your students' needs.

Using the course from start to finish

You can, of course, use *Business Result Second Edition* conventionally, starting at *Unit 1* and working your way through each unit in turn. If you do so, you will find it works well. Each section of the unit is related thematically to the others, and there is a degree of recycling and a steady progression towards overall competence, culminating in the *Talking point*. Timing will inevitably vary, but allow approximately four classroom hours for each unit. You will need more time if you intend to do the *Practice file* activities in class.

The 'flexible' option

Business Result Second Edition is written in a way that recognizes that many business English courses vary greatly in length. With this in mind, teachers can use *Business Result Second Edition* in a modular way. Although each unit has a logical progression, you will find that all the sections are essentially free-standing and can be used independently of the rest of the unit.

This modular approach provides the flexibility that business English teachers need when planning their course. Teachers might want to choose the sections or unit topics that are the most relevant and interesting to them and their students.

Online practice and teacher resources

For students

The *Online practice* gives your students additional language practice of the *Student's Book* content. For more information, see page 5 of the *Student's Book*.

For teachers

As well as providing access to all of the student online practice exercises, the Learning Management System (LMS) provides an invaluable and time-saving feature for teachers.

You can monitor your students' progress and all of their results at the touch of a button. You can also print off and use student reports on their progress.

A user manual for how to use the LMS can be found in the teacher resources in the *Online practice*.

Downloadable resources for teachers

In the teacher resources in the *Online practice* are a number of downloadable resources for teachers to use to complement the *Student's Book*. These include:

- Photocopiable worksheets for every unit
- Progress tests for every unit
- Business cards for role-plays
- Class audio
- Class video

Photocopiable worksheets

New for *Business Result Second Edition* are the photocopiable worksheets. These provide extra communicative practice, often in the form of a game, for every *Working with words*, *Language at work*, and *Business communication* section from the *Student's Book*.

There are suggestions in the *Teacher's Book* for when to use these worksheets in class. All of the worksheets, as well as the answer key, can be downloaded and photocopied from the teacher resources in the *Online practice*.

Photocopiable Progress tests

These can be administered at the end of each unit in order to assess your students' progress and allow you, the student or the head of training to keep track of students' overall ability.

Each test is divided into two sections. The first section tests the vocabulary, grammar and key expressions from the unit. This section is scored out of 30 and students will need about 30 minutes to complete the questions.

The second section is a speaking test. In this section students are given a speaking task that resembles one of the speaking activities in the unit. These are mostly set up as pairwork activities in the form of role-plays, discussions or presentations.

Marking criteria is provided to help you assess students' performance in the speaking test. It requires students to perform five functions in the speaking test, and you can grade each of the five functions using a scoring system of 0, 1 or 2, giving a final score out of 10.

The speaking test role-plays can also be used as extra classroom practice without necessarily making use of the marking criteria.

All of the tests, and the answer keys, can be downloaded from the teacher resources in the *Online practice*.

Business cards

There is a set of downloadable business cards in the teacher resources in the *Online practice*.

The business cards are particularly useful to use in role-play situations from the *Student's Book* if you have students from the same company and they are required to exchange information about their company. You will find suggestions of when to use the business cards in the teacher notes of the *Teacher's Book*.

Class audio and video

All of the class audio and the videos for the *Viewpoint* lessons can be streamed or downloaded from the teacher resources in the *Online practice*.

Alternatively, class audio can be played from the audio CD and the videos can be played from the DVD that is found in the *Teacher's Book* pack.

How to access the *Online practice*

For students

Students use the access card on the inside front cover of the *Student's Book*. This contains an access code to unlock the content in the *Online practice*.

For teachers

Teachers need to go to **www.oxfordlearn.com** and either **register** or **sign in**. Members of the Oxford Teacher's Club can use their existing sign in details.

Then click on **Register an organization** and follow the instructions. Note that if you are not part of an organization, or you don't have an authorization code from your institution, you will need to click on **Apply for an organization account**. You will then be asked to supply some information. If you don't have an institution, then put your own name next to Institution name.

Teacher's website

Additional teacher resources can be found at **www.oup.com/elt/teacher/businessresult.**

1 Working life

Context

The topic of *Working life* gives the students the tools to present themselves and their company to clients and competitors. Anybody who works or plans to work in business will need a certain amount of vocabulary to describe a company, including its main areas of business, its working activities and their role in the company. Not only is it important to find out about a contact's company for practical business reasons, but it is also a subject of interest to most business people, and so will be a topic of conversation in many business situations; particularly in initial meetings and setting up contacts.

Social interaction in business is crucial for the forging of good relationships and making new contacts. Cultural differences can lead to misunderstandings if business people do not use the appropriate expressions and intonation when reacting to speakers in their initial exchanges.

In this unit, students will learn how to describe their companies and their role in their company. They will also have the opportunity to practise a very important social aspect of business interaction – reacting to speakers, sounding interested and extending a conversation.

The *Talking point* offers students the opportunity to discuss the area of networking, whilst providing the opportunity to develop their fluency using some of the language from the unit.

Starting point

Do the first question with the whole class. Give them cues if they are hesitant: *Is it a big or small company? Is it a manufacturing or a service company? Is it local, national or international?* The second question can be done in pairs before whole-class feedback, or with the whole class. The third question can be done individually initially, then students can get into pairs or small groups to compare answers and finally discuss as a whole class. Encourage students to develop their answers.

PRE-WORK LEARNERS Ask students to think about their ideal working life. Ask questions about it, for example, *What kind of business or organization would you like to work for? Where would you prefer to spend most of your working day? Would you prefer to work on your own or with colleagues/clients?* You could ask students to discuss the questions in small groups and then report back to the whole class.

Working with words

Exercise 1

Allow students a few minutes to look at the question and prompts before speaking. Elicit what they know about online sites. You could do the first prompt as a model, for example, a company website could include the company logo, photos of the buildings or products, endorsements from clients or customers, the company contact details, some information about the company itself and about the staff.

Possible answers

A company website: logo, clients/customers, contact details, information on company and staff
A personal webpage: probably includes a profile, blog/vlog, photos
A social media site such as Facebook or LinkedIn: contacts, friends, endorsements, news
A brochure or publication such as a conference programme: background information, future plans, conference schedule, speakers at a conference

Exercise 2

Ask students to read the four profiles and answer the questions. Tell students it's not necessary to understand all the words, only the general sense. Provide feedback on answers with the whole class.

Answers

1 In-balance; high quality training courses on employment law, health and safety, and using mobile technologies in marketing
2 Howard Bright and Fey de Boutilier. (Normally when we talk about our jobs, we mean full-time jobs. We generally only state specifically if they are part-time. This is the reason the answers for Howard Bright and Fey de Boutilier are inferred from the text rather than explicitly stated, as in the case of the remaining profiles.)
3 Tasia Clifford and Emrann Bhatt.

Exercise 3

Tell students to read the profiles again and complete the table. Let them compare their answers with a partner. Provide feedback on answers with the whole class.

Suggested answers

	Job(s)	Colleagues and clients	Main area(s) of business	Workplace activities
Tasia	business lawyer and trainer	managers and businesses	employment law and health and safety	advising managers and businesses in two areas of law
Emrann	marketing consultant and trainer	small-to-medium sized business owners	marketing and online marketing	developing marketing strategies / running courses on using mobile technologies in marketing
Fey	customer service representative	multinational corporations to individual customers	customer service	the booking process, from initial enquiries to taking bookings

Exercise 4

After the pairwork, ask two or three students to report back to the whole class.

PRE-WORK LEARNERS Ask students to work in small groups to discuss their ideal job, for example, *What would the job be? Would they prefer to work part-time or full-time? If they worked part-time, what else would they do?* Ask them to give reasons for their choices.

Exercise 5

Elicit the answer to the first sentence with the whole class, then ask them to complete the other sentences individually. Let them compare answers in pairs before doing whole-class feedback.

Answers

1 with 2 for 3 of 4 of 5 in 6 as 7 in 8 with

PRONUNCIATION Write *work with* on the board and ask which word or syllable is stressed. Explain that we link the verb and preposition in the verb phrases, i.e. that they sound like one word and that the stress is generally on the verb, noun or adjective in the phrase. Show the link *work with*, /ˈwɜːkwɪð/

Then ask them to do the same for the other verb phrases, encouraging them to say them aloud to see if the pronunciation sounds correct. Check answers with the whole class.

Answers

1 <u>work</u> with /ˈwɜːkwɪð/
2 res<u>pon</u>sible for /rɪˈspɒnsəblfɔː(r)/
3 con<u>sists</u> of /kənˈsɪstsɒv/
4 in <u>charge</u> of /ɪnˈtʃɑːdʒɒv/
5 <u>special</u>ize in /ˈspeʃəlaɪzɪn/
6 <u>work</u> as /wɜːkəz/
7 <u>work</u> in /wɜːkɪn/
8 <u>deal</u> with /diːlwɪð/

You could then ask students in pairs to read the complete sentences in **5** aloud, focusing on correct word stress and linking. Monitor, and correct their pronunciation where necessary.

Exercise 6

Tell students to read the sentences in **5** again and match them to the categories a–d. Remind them that some of the sentences can refer to more than one category.

Answers

a Job: 6
b Colleagues and clients: 1, 4
c Areas of business: 2, 5, 7
d Workplace activities: 2, 3, 4, 7, 8

Further practice

If students need more practice, go to *Practice file 1* on page 106 of the *Student's Book*.

Exercise 7

Students work in pairs to discuss their job. Refer students to the *Tip*. Remind them to use the verb phrases from **5**. Monitor, and ask students to self-correct if you hear mistakes in pronunciation.

PRE-WORK LEARNERS Ask students to imagine they work for a (real) well-known company. You could do this activity as a further practice exercise in the next lesson and ask students to research the necessary information (revenue, employees, etc.) on the Internet.

Exercise 8

Students work individually to create a profile for themselves and their job for their company website. If students are all from the same company or haven't started work, follow the suggestions in the 'Pre-work learners' section in **7**. To provide a model, ask students to quickly read the profiles in **2** again to give them an idea of what to write. Then either allow students time to prepare this writing activity or set it as homework.

Photocopiable worksheet

Download and photocopy *Unit 1 Working with words worksheet* from the teacher resources in the *Online practice*.

Language at work

Exercise 1

Students in pairs tell each other when and why they have given a short presentation about themselves and their work or studies.

PRE-WORK LEARNERS Ask students to imagine when and why they would be asked to give a presentation to a group of people.

Exercise 2

▶ **1.1** Before they listen to the conversation, ask students to read questions 1–6 and think about what sort of information they are listening for. Then ask them to answer the questions in pairs.

Answers
1 a training course in online marketing
2 give a short presentation about themselves
3 a medical charity
4 fundraising projects and advertising
5 in Paris
6 She needs to learn about online marketing.

Exercise 3

▶ **1.1** Ask students to read the sentences and try to complete them. Let them check their answers with a partner. Play the conversation again and tell students to complete the sentences with the missing verbs. Students can check the answers in pairs and then check with whole-class feedback.

Answers
2 deal
3 'm, running
4 'm living, working
5 are, taking
6 advertises
7 are reading, watching
8 don't know

Exercise 4

As this is the first time students may have done this type of grammatical analysis, it is probably better to guide the whole class through the activity rather than work in pairs. Be aware that this *Language point* focuses on two areas – present simple and present continuous, and then adverbs frequently used with each.

First of all, ask the students to complete explanations a–f in the first part of the *Language point* with *simple* or *continuous*. They then match the sentences in **3** to the explanations. Ask students to read the *Tip* and then find the adverbs in the sentences in **3** to complete the second part of the *Language point*.

Answers
b continuous – Sentences 3 and 5   e continuous – Sentence 4
c simple – Sentence 1   f simple – Sentence 8
d continuous – Sentence 7
Adverbs of frequency: often, usually
Adverbs of time: currently, today, these days (note that only two of these answers are required)

Grammar reference

If students need more information, go to *Grammar reference* on page 107 of the *Student's Book*.

Exercise 5

Tell students to underline the correct tense and add the adverb in the correct place. Check answers in whole-class feedback.

Answers
1 What <u>are you working</u> on at the moment? / At the moment, what <u>are you working</u> on?
2 We <u>have</u> offices in over 20 countries.
3 More and more of our customers <u>are ordering</u> our goods online these days. / These days, more and more of our customers <u>are ordering</u> our goods online.
4 I'm normally <u>responsible</u> for everyone else's travel arrangements. / Normally, I'<u>m responsible</u> for everyone else's travel arrangements.
5 We <u>aren't doing</u> any business in Brazil until we can all speak Portuguese.
6 Overall, the economic climate <u>is improving</u>.
7 My company <u>is</u> currently <u>trying</u> to increase its trade in China. / Currently, my company <u>is trying</u> to increase its trade in China.
8 I'<u>m doing</u> this course because I <u>don't understand</u> Excel software.
9 <u>Do you</u> often <u>give</u> presentations in your job?

EXTENSION Tell students to think of three or four questions using the present simple or present continuous to ask classmates about their normal routines, and what they are doing now that's different or temporary. Students then stand up and move round the room asking their questions. Two or three can report back what they found out to the whole class.

Further practice

If students need more practice, go to *Practice file 1* on page 107 of the *Student's Book*.

Exercise 6

Give students time to work individually to prepare their presentation. If students are all from the same company, you could suggest they imagine their ideal job. You could ask students to research real companies on the Internet and describe a job they have read about. You might like to provide a model first, describing your own job.

PRE-WORK LEARNERS Ask students to imagine they work for a (real) well-known company. Ask them to think of a job they would like to do and a project they could be working on. Ask them to describe these to a partner.

Exercise 7

Students take turns to give their presentations. This can be done to the whole class or in pairs or small groups. The person or people listening should take notes on what the presenter said and ask follow-up questions.

EXTENSION Put the students in new pairs. They should report to their new partner about their first partner's company. Make sure they use the third person forms correctly. You could then ask two or three students to report back to the class.

Photocopiable worksheet

Download and photocopy *Unit 1 Language at work worksheet* from the teacher resources in the *Online practice*.

Practically speaking

Exercise 1

Start by asking students how you show interest when you listen to someone in different situations, for example, the sounds you make (if any), body language, eye contact, etc. Explain that these can be different in different cultures and ask students if they have noticed any differences themselves.

Exercise 2

▶ **1.2** Explain that students are going to listen to a conversation. Before they listen, ask them to guess the answers. Play the listening and let students compare answers in pairs before checking answers with the whole class. Ask students to notice how the listener shows interest in what the speaker says.

Answers
1 b 2 a 3 c

Exercise 3

▶ **1.3** Play the listening once. Ask students if they can hear the sentence stress and the rise and fall in intonation. Then play the listening again, pausing after each sentence, asking students to mark the stress. Point out that it is important for your voice to go up and down in order to show that you are interested in what someone says.

When showing interest it is normal for the voice to rise and fall. Write the phrase *That sounds interesting.* and mark the stress and intonation.

Exercise 4

If necessary, play the listening again. Tell students that one important way to show interest is to ask a follow-up question or find a connection. Ask students what words the listener uses.

Answers
1 Suggesting keeping in contact: 3 c
2 Finding a connection: 2 a
3 Asking a question: 1 b

Exercise 5

Students work individually to write the sentences. Then in pairs they say their sentences and their partner reacts, showing interest and extending the conversation. Monitor and make sure the students respond using the target expressions from **2** with the correct intonation and a technique from **4**.

PRE-WORK LEARNERS Ask students to write five sentences about their lives, their studies, their hobbies and interests, their family or friends.

Business communication

Exercise 1

Tell students to discuss the questions with a partner.

PRE-WORK LEARNERS Ask students if they ever go to conferences or meetings with people who have similar interests. Ask if they think these events are useful or not.

Exercise 2

▶ **1.4** Play the extracts from two different conversations once. Let students compare answers in pairs and then check with the whole class.

Answers
Luc Akele: Area manager. In charge of sub-Saharan operations. Oversees projects. Reports to sponsors.
Jo Johansson: Deals with fund applications.
Walter Mayer: Medical donations programme. Handles inter-governmental work. Negotiating.

Exercise 3

▶ **1.4** Play the listening again and ask students to tick the person who says each expression. Let them compare answers in pairs. If necessary, listen again and pause after each expression to elicit the answer.

Answers

Conversation 1	Hannah	Jo	Luc
1 I want you to meet …	✓		
2 Nice to meet you.		✓	
3 What do you do, exactly?		✓	
4 I'm afraid I have to go now.			✓
5 It was nice meeting you, too.		✓	
6 I'd like to keep in contact.			✓
7 Do you have a card?			✓

Conversation 2	Dr Mayer	Hiroko
8 Let me introduce myself.		✓
9 I'm delighted to meet you.	✓	
10 Please, call me Walter.	✓	
11 I'm very pleased to meet you, too.		✓
12 Here's my card.	✓	
13 Which part of Japan are you from?	✓	
14 It was nice meeting you.		✓
15 I look forward to hearing from you.	✓	

Remind students that we use 'actually' to mean 'in fact' NOT ‘at the moment / right now'. It's a polite way to correct or contradict someone:

Which part of Japan are you from? **Actually**, *I'm from Brazil.*

EXTENSION To practise the use of *actually*, ask students to write three things they know are untrue about their partner. Students take turns to ask a question or make a statement about their partner. Their partner has to correct or contradict them. For example:

A *So what's your position in the Marketing Department?*
B *Actually, I'm in the Sales Department.*

Exercise 4

Ask students to look at the *Key expressions* and decide which are more formal. Then, in pairs, students decide which conversation from **3** is more formal and say why.

> **Answers**
> Conversation 2 is more formal. Expressions such as 'Let me introduce myself.' and 'I'm delighted to meet you.' are used in more formal situations. However, this doesn't mean that conversation 1 is informal. It is simply less formal or neutral in tone.

Further practice

If students need more practice, go to *Practice file 1* on page 106 of the *Student's Book*.

Exercise 5

Students take turns practising with a partner. You could set the exercise up by asking for an expression for each stage of the flow chart. You can use the downloadable business cards from the teacher resources in the *Online practice* for this activity.

Exercise 6

Divide the students into groups of four. Tell them to introduce their partner to the others in the group. They can then make a different group of four and introduce each other again.

ONE-TO-ONE Tell the student to introduce him/herself to you. If you have time, ask them to imagine a real colleague and introduce him/her to you as well.

Photocopiable worksheet

Download and photocopy *Unit 1 Business communication worksheet* from the teacher resources in the *Online practice*.

Talking point

Discussion

Exercise 1

Tell students to read the information on Speed networking and discuss the questions with a partner. Provide whole-class feedback by asking one or two pairs to report.

> **Possible answers**
> Advantages: make a large number of contacts in a very short time, can choose which contacts to follow up and which not to. Disadvantages: can become boring to repeat yourself so many times, can talk to a lot of people who aren't worth developing as business contacts.

Exercise 2

Ask students to think of their own job and decide how useful speed networking would be. Ask them to discuss their answers with a partner, giving reasons.

PRE-WORK LEARNERS Ask students to discuss when they could use speed networking in their lives. How could having lots of contacts with other people with a similar interest be useful?

Task

Exercise 1

Check students understand they can talk about themselves or choose a person from the role cards on page 136 of the *Student's Book*. You could do a trial run, modelling the activity for the whole class with information about yourself, covering the three bullet points.

Exercise 2

Ask students to stand up and begin by introducing themselves to someone in the class and carrying on the conversation as instructed. After they have talked for four minutes, they fill in the table with the person's information, score the person they were talking to and give the reason for their score.

Exercise 3

After a total of five minutes, give a signal or tell students to move on to another person. Students speak to three people in total to complete the score card.

ONE-TO-ONE You could take the roles of several different people at the event, and your student must introduce him/herself to you over and over again. You could ask him/her to change roles and introduce him/herself as one of the people from the role cards on page 136, or do the activity as revision at the start of the next lesson.

Exercise 4

Finally, each student tells the class about the most useful contact they made and the reason for their choice.

Progress test

Download and photocopy *Unit 1 Progress test* and *Speaking test* from the teacher resources in the *Online practice*.

2 Work–life balance

Context

The topic of *Work–life balance* gives students the language to describe how their job impacts on their life and whether they feel they have achieved a good work–life balance. If anyone works or plans to work in business, they will need specific vocabulary to describe their job and how they feel about their working conditions. This allows people to compare working conditions in different companies and discuss how they feel their job affects their family life, leisure time and perhaps even health.

Social interaction in business is crucial for the forging of good relationships. For a business to be successful, it is essential to make and keep useful contacts. To do this, students need to be able to exchange details accurately and efficiently.

In this unit, students will learn how to describe the terms and conditions of employment in their jobs and how they feel about them. They will also have the opportunity to practise an important social aspect of interaction in their company and with contacts – saying 'yes' when responding to requests.

The *Talking point* offers students the opportunity to develop their fluency by playing a game, *Corridor conversations*, using the language from the unit.

Starting point

Do the first question with the whole class. Give them cues if they are hesitant: *What do you think would be a good work–life balance? How many hours do you expect to work each day?* Ask the students to discuss the second question with a partner before whole-class feedback. Encourage students to develop their answers.

Background information for 2

The USA seems to have one of the highest 'long-hours' cultures, with some employers expecting employees to work every day, if required. In general, working hours throughout Asia are longer than those worked in Europe or the USA, while in countries like India a working week of 50–60 hours is not unusual. Life in Australia has the reputation for being laid-back, but working hours there are longer than in Europe and many people don't take all of their annual leave.

Working with words

Exercise 1

Ask students to work in pairs and discuss the question. Do whole-class feedback.

Possible answers
Because tired workers are generally less efficient and less happy in their jobs. They may decide to look for a less stressful/tiring job, so a company might lose essential staff.

Exercise 2

Ask students to read the text quickly. Tell them it is not necessary to understand all the words, only the general sense of each section. Provide feedback on answers with the whole class.

Answers
1 Working hours
2 Holiday
3 Family and health

Exercise 3

Ask students to discuss the question in pairs. Do whole-class feedback, with students coming up with reasons.

Possible answers
Good: flexitime, home-working allowed, good holidays
Bad: shorter paternity leave, limited when it can be taken

Exercise 4

Refer students to the *Tip*. Show them where to find the answer to the first definition in the text, then ask them to find the words for the other definitions individually. Let them compare answers with a partner before doing whole-class feedback.

PRONUNCIATION Ask students to say the words aloud and mark the stress on the compound words. They take turns to practise in pairs by one student giving a definition and the other giving the answer. Monitor and correct pronunciation where necessary.

Exercise 5

Ask students to read the text in **2** again and use the information to give answers.

EXTENSION Working in pairs, students practise by taking turns to be the manager and employee, giving answers to the questions.

Exercise 6

Give students a few minutes to think of answers to the questions, that are true for their company. Tell them to do the exercise and then ask one or two pairs to answer the questions in whole-class feedback.

ALTERNATIVE If all the students work for the same company, ask them to find information about different (real) companies from the Internet. Then ask them to work with a partner who researched a different company to answer the questions in **5**.

PRE-WORK LEARNERS Ask students to imagine they work for a (real) well-known company. They could think up the terms and conditions for the company.

You could do this activity as a further practice exercise in the next lesson and ask students to research the necessary information on a (real) company on the Internet for homework.

Exercise 7

Get the students to swap roles and practise the questions and answers in **6**. Do whole-class feedback by comparing answers from different pairs.

Further practice

If students need more practice, go to *Practice file 2* on page 108 of the *Student's Book*.

Exercise 8

▶ **2.1** Allow students time to study the table. Ask them what kind of information they need to listen for. You may want to check students understand *time off in lieu* before they listen. Play the listening and ask students to complete the table. They can then compare notes in pairs before listening a second time. Check answers with the whole class. Ask students how similar the terms and conditions are at their companies.

Exercise 9

Students work in pairs. Monitor and ask students to self-correct if you hear mistakes in pronunciation.

PRE-WORK LEARNERS Ask students to compare the speakers' responses and decide if they would like to work for either company. Ask them to give reasons for their answer.

DICTIONARY SKILLS

Write the words *employer*, *employee* and *employ* on the board and point out that they are all from the same 'word family'. Students look up the words in a good monolingual dictionary. Ask them how the part of speech is indicated in the dictionary, i.e. *Is it a verb, adjective or noun? How is the main stress on the word indicated? What examples are given for each word?* (N.B. the answers will depend on the particular dictionary they use.) Then ask them to search in the dictionary for other words in the same family as *work*.

Possible answers
employ (v), employer (n), employee (n), employment (n), employed (adj), unemployed (adj), under-employed (adj), work (v), worker (n), home-working (n), workplace (n), work experience (n), work-related (adj), overworked (adj), hard-working (adj)

Photocopiable worksheet

Download and photocopy *Unit 2 Working with words worksheet* from the teacher resources in the *Online practice*.

Language at work

Exercise 1

Students individually complete the quiz and add up their score.

PRE-WORK LEARNERS Either write these new statements on the board or dictate them. Tell students to score the statements as instructed in the quiz:

2 I never **think about spending** extra time studying at the weekend.

3 This year I **don't intend to work** during the college holidays.

4 I always organize my study schedule **to make sure** I have free time in the evening.

Exercise 2

In pairs, students discuss their scores to decide if they agree with the results and compare answers to see if their ideas of a good work–life balance are similar.

PRE-WORK LEARNERS Ask students to think about their own answers and decide whether they think they have a good study–life balance. Ask them to think of one way they could improve it. They can then compare their answers with a partner.

Exercise 3

Ask students to read the sentences in **1** again, looking at the verb forms in bold. Then ask them to complete the *Language point*, choosing the correct words in italics and writing the relevant sentence number.

Students then compare answers in pairs, before whole-class feedback. Highlight the patterns for each category.

> **Answers**
> a *to* + infinitive 5
> b the *-ing* form 2
> c *to* + infinitive 4
> d The *-ing* form 1
> e *To* + infinitive 3

Exercise 4

Ask students to look at the information in the *Language point*, and answer the question in pairs. Give feedback on answers with the whole class, eliciting why students' answers are not correct if they choose the wrong option.

> **Answers**
> *to* + infinitive: want, agree, it's difficult, would like, plan, I'm pleased, decide
> the *-ing* form: responsible for, look forward to, involve, interested in, enjoy

EXTENSION You could ask students to choose four or five of the verbs and phrases and give an example of each that is true for themselves for practice.

Grammar reference

If students need more information, go to *Grammar reference* on page 109 of the *Student's Book*.

Exercise 5

Refer students to the *Tip* and ask them to read the questions to decide if the verb patterns in italics are correct or not. In pairs, they can compare answers and correct any that are wrong. Check answers in whole-class feedback.

> **Answers**
> 1 ✓
> 2 ✓
> 3 What percentage of your time consists of *working* in teams and what percentage on your own?
> 4 ✓
> 5 Do you plan *to take* unpaid leave at any time in the next three years?
> 6 ✓
> 7 Would you like *to manage* your own working hours?
> 8 If you had flexitime, would you decide *to start* work earlier or later in the day?

Further practice

If students need more practice, go to *Practice file 2* on page 109 of the *Student's Book*.

Exercise 6

In pairs, students ask and answer the questions in **5** about their own working hours. Tell them to give reasons for their answers.

PRE-WORK LEARNERS Ask students to prepare their own answers to the questions in **5** about a company they know, an imaginary company, or about their present situation. Then they can do the exercise in pairs.

Exercise 7

Ask students to work individually to write three questions for the survey. Then, in pairs, they take turns to ask their questions.

> **Possible answers**
> 1 Do you plan to take all your annual leave this year?
> 2 Is it difficult for you to take a full hour for your lunch every day?
> 3 Do you like working in a big office?

PRE-WORK LEARNERS Ask students to write three questions about their studies. Tell them to work with a partner to ask and answer their questions.

> **Possible answers**
> 1 Is it difficult for you to organize a study schedule? Why/Why not?
> 2 Do you like revising on your own, or discussing questions with other students?
> 3 What do you plan to do during the college holiday: work, take a holiday or study?

Photocopiable worksheet

Download and photocopy *Unit 2 Language at work worksheet* from the teacher resources in the *Online practice*.

Practically speaking

Exercise 1

Start by asking students if they feel they always have to say 'yes' when their boss or colleagues ask them to do something at work. Have they ever said 'yes' when they really wanted to say 'no'? Ask them why it's sometimes difficult to say 'no' to certain people. Ask them to think of situations where they have found it hard or impossible to say 'no'.

PRE-WORK LEARNERS Ask students to discuss the questions below, and give real life examples if possible. Ask them to give reasons for their answers.

When a friend or classmate asks you to do something for them, do you always say yes?

When your teacher asks you to do extra work, or give extra help in class, do you always say yes?

Is it more difficult to say no to your teacher or your friend/ classmate?

Exercise 2

▶ **2.2** Explain that students are going to listen to four conversations where someone is making a request. Play the listening and let students compare answers in pairs before checking answers with the whole class.

> **Answers**
> Conversation 1: b
> Conversation 2: d
> Conversation 3: a
> Conversation 4: c

Exercise 3

▶ **2.2** Ask students if they can remember any of the ways the speakers said 'yes'. Then play the listening again for students to match the answers 1–4 to the requests a–d. Check answers with the whole class.

> **Answers**
> **1** b **2** c **3** a **4** d

Exercise 4

Elicit the answer from the whole class. Ask students who they think they can/can't use this answer with.

> **Answer**
> Yes, I suppose so.
> Perhaps don't use it with your manager.

PRONUNCIATION Ask students to listen to the responses again and notice the difference in intonation between the positive answers and the less positive one. Ask students to practise saying the sentences.

Exercise 5

Students take turns to be the manager/colleague making the request and the colleague saying 'yes' in each of the situations. Monitor and make sure the students respond using the target expressions in **3** with the correct intonation.

Business communication

Exercise 1

Ask students to tick the information they keep about work contacts.

> **Possible answers**
> email, website, mobile number, picture, work address, office number. others: working hours in the office / at home

PRE-WORK LEARNERS Ask students to think about the social media platforms they are on. Ask them to look at the list and say what information they and their contacts have in their profiles. Ask them if there is any information they decided not to put in their profile and ask them to give reasons.

Exercise 2

Students discuss the answer in pairs and then check with the whole class.

> **Possible answer**
> Not very difficult. It can be organized on our phones/computers for us.

Exercise 3

▶ **2.3** Ask students to read the headings and decide what information they are listening for. Play the conversation and ask students to complete the information. Let them compare answers in pairs. If necessary, play the listening again.

> **Answers**
> Name: Leif Gunnarson
> Office: 0046 967 55 6745
> Email: leif.gunnarson@sbnshipping.se
> Company website: www.SBNshipping.se/sales

Exercise 4

▶ **2.3** Students work in pairs. Give them time to do the matching exercise, then play the conversation again to check.

> **Answers**
> **1** g **2** h **3** b **4** e **5** d **6** a **7** f **8** c

Tell students that when they need to check or clarify details such as spelling and numbers, they should stress the difference.

| Further practice
| If students need more practice, go to *Practice file 2* on
| page 108 of the *Student's Book*.

Exercise 5

Students prepare for **6** individually. You can use the downloadable business cards from the teacher resources in the *Online practice* for this exercise. Monitor, checking students have written the information correctly and checking pronunciation for spelling.

Students may need to revise how to pronounce the letters in the English alphabet. Put the phonetic symbols on the board and get the students to decide which sounds the letters go under.

/eɪ/	/iː/	/e/	/aɪ/	/əʊ/	/uː/	/ɑː/
a	b	f	i	o	q	r
h	c	l	y		u	
j	d	m			w	
k	e	n				
	g	s				
	p	x				
	t	z (UK)				
	v					
	z (US)					

Ask students to imagine they work in a (real) well-known company and to give the information for someone who works there.

Exercise 6

Ask students to take turns to ask for and give details using the prompts. Monitor and check the information is correct.

Suggested answers
1 Can I have / Can you tell me your last name?
2 What's your/his/her number?
3 Could you give me your/his/her email?
4 Do you have the company web address?

Exercise 7

Refer students to the *Key expressions* for language to help them with the task. Students work in pairs, A and B. Student A turns to page 137, and B to page 142. Students can then practise the conversations with the information on their pages.

Photocopiable worksheet

Download and photocopy *Unit 2 Business communication worksheet* from the teacher resources in the *Online practice*.

Talking point

The objective of this game is to practise the language for this unit in a light-hearted context. Make sure you have a dice for each group and counters for each student.

Check students understand both the rules and the navigation of the game. You could do a trial run of one or two 'goes' with the whole class. Monitor during the game, checking the instructions are being followed correctly. Help with answers and pronunciation if necessary.

Possible answers
2 Do you like working in a team? / Do you like working alone?
3 Hello. What's your name?
4 Is your phone number 07789925566 or 07789926655?
5 In your job, is it difficult to take time off?
7 Next year, do you plan to take any unpaid leave?
8 What do you enjoy doing in your leisure time?
9 How often do you travel abroad for work?
11 What does your department deal with?
12 What are your main responsibilities?
13 Can you give me your mobile number?
14 Tell me about your job.
15 Can I just check your email address? Is it …?
16 Can I have your company website address?
17 Do you like football? Do you support a team?
19 Sorry, I didn't catch that. How do you spell your name?

To make sure that the student gets the maximum practice in the language in the game, give him/her the chance to answer first each time. If he/she answers correctly on his/her turn, he/she proceeds as per the normal rules. If he/she answers correctly on your turn, you must stay in the same place.

Write the following on the board for students to refer to when they get to the relevant squares:

5 In your studies, is it difficult to …?
11 Ask another player about his/her favourite subject.
12 Ask another player about the job he/she plans to do.
14 Move to the nearest player's square. Ask him/her to describe his/her ideal job.
16 Move to the nearest player's square. Ask for and check the web address of a well-known company from his/her country.

Progress test

Download and photocopy *Unit 2 Progress test* and *Speaking test* from the teacher resources in the *Online practice*.

3 Projects

Unit content

By the end of this unit, students will be able to

- talk about projects
- talk about the progress of a project using the present perfect and past simple
- give short answers
- update and delegate tasks.

Context

The topic of *Projects* gives students the language to describe the stages and progress of a project, working in a team. It is clear that the initial planning stage of any project is vital, and that effective planning means a smooth running project. Not only is it important to plan carefully, but it is also essential to think about possible scenarios where the project does not run to the initial plan, for whatever reason, and where effective changes need to be made quickly and efficiently. Correct use of the tenses in the unit make clear which stages are complete and which are still in progress.

Social interaction between colleagues is crucial for effective teamwork in both formal and informal situations. Cultural differences can lead to misunderstandings if colleagues do not use the appropriate expressions, and inadvertently sounding rude or abrupt may cause preventable problems within the team.

In this unit students will learn how to describe setting up, organizing and staging a project. They will have the opportunity to practise an important aspect of personal interaction in a team – responding with short answers using auxiliary verbs. They will also practise updating and delegating tasks.

In the *Talking point*, students have the opportunity to give a presentation on the planning of an event and give alternatives for different scenarios.

Starting point

Do the first question with the whole class. Give them cues if they are hesitant: *What do you need to do before starting a project? Should you do anything while the project is in progress? What would be useful to do after a project?* The second and third questions can be done with the whole class or in pairs before whole-class feedback. Encourage students to develop their answers.

Possible answers

1 Make sure the project is well-organized – spend time planning by working out the stages and timings, and resourcing the project efficiently. Set up the team, making sure everyone knows what they should be doing. Have regular updates to check each stage is progressing on schedule.

PRE-WORK LEARNERS Ask students how they go about organizing a study assignment or project. How do they find out the information they need for the topic? What do they do before they start writing? How do they plan each stage? How do they make sure they hit the deadline? Ask them to think of the last big assignment or project they did and evaluate how successfully they tackled it and what they can improve on.

Working with words

Exercise 1

Ask students to discuss the questions with a partner. Elicit from the students what they know about any charities and how they work with companies. Make sure they understand *to volunteer / a volunteer / volunteerism*. Some information they may come up with:

- different types of charities – medical, social, educational, international, national, local
- how charities raise money – donations, events
- who might need help from charities – those in poverty, those displaced due to a natural disaster
- how many people work for them / volunteer for them.

Exercise 2

Ask students to read sentences 1–4 and then the article. Tell students it's not necessary to understand all the words, only the general sense. Provide feedback on answers with the whole class.

Answers

1 T   2 F   3 T   4 F

Exercise 3

Ask students to compare answers in small groups. After the group work, provide feedback with the whole class.

PRE-WORK LEARNERS Ask students to think about a (real) company they know of whose staff take part in volunteer projects. If they don't know of one, they could suggest how one or two well-known companies could set some projects up.

Exercise 4

You could check the first answer with the whole class and then ask students to complete the other sentences individually. Let them compare answers with a partner before doing whole-class feedback.

Answers

2	budget	6	objectives
3	teamwork	7	milestone
4	updates	8	resources
5	deadline		

Exercise 5

▶ **3.1** Ask students to quickly read the answers in **4** again. Then play the listening and ask them to answer the questions. If necessary, play the listening again for them to note what Samira said about each part of the project. Students compare answers in pairs before whole-class feedback.

Answers

1
deadline schedule resources budget teamwork updates
2
(deadline): the end of the week
(schedule): they fell behind schedule because of the holiday
(resources): at first it was hard to know how to allocate these
(budget): she has stayed within it
(teamwork): it's essential
(update): she gets updates every two days

Exercise 6

▶ **3.1** Ask students to try to complete the phrases from memory. Play the listening again for them to check.

Answers

1	meet	6	allocate
2	behind	7	within
3	up	8	delegate
4	on	9	on
5	ahead of	10	get

Exercise 7

Tell students to cover the phrases in column A in **6**. Working with a partner, they take turns to test them using the definitions in column B. Monitor, checking their answers and pronunciation.

Further practice

If students need more practice, go to *Practice file 3* on page 110 of the *Student's Book*.

Exercise 8

Give students time to read the problems and think about solutions. Refer them to the *Tip*. Ask them to come up with at least one solution for each problem, with a partner. They can then compare their answers with another pair's and decide which is best. Check answers with the whole class.

Possible answers

2 They are currently over budget but need to stay on budget.
3 The project lacks resources. The manager needs to allocate resources and delegate tasks to other people.
4 The manager needs to improve communication by getting regular updates from the team.

EXTENSION Check students' understanding of *in time / on time* in the *Tip* by asking them the following questions. *What time do you start work? Are you always on time? When was the last time you took a flight? Did you arrive at the airport in time to do some shopping before checking in?*

DICTIONARY SKILLS

Write *schedule* on the board. Ask students to think of words that go with *schedule*, for example, *be on schedule, fall/be behind schedule, get back on schedule, keep to schedule, have a busy schedule*, etc. Ask students to find at least two collocations in their dictionaries for the following: *budget, deadline, track, update*.

Answers

be on / go over budget, meet/miss a deadline, be on track / keep track of something, ask for / have a regular update

Exercise 9

Students work individually initially, making notes on each prompt. Then they take turns describing their project. The student listening can ask questions to clarify any plans, possible problems, etc. Monitor and ask students to self-correct if you hear mistakes in pronunciation.

PRE-WORK LEARNERS Ask students to imagine they work for a (real) well-known company and think of a project. You could do this activity as a further practice exercise in the next lesson and ask them to research the necessary information (plans for future developments, how these are organized, etc.) on the Internet.

Photocopiable worksheet

Download and photocopy *Unit 3 Working with words worksheet* from the teacher resources in the *Online practice*.

Language at work

Exercise 1

Ask students to read the chart. Make sure they understand what it shows. You may need to check vocabulary, *equipment, supplier, collate, install,* and the abbreviation, *depts.,* in the 'Stage' column.

Possible answer

It gives information about what each stage is and when it should be completed.

PRE-WORK LEARNERS Ask students: *How do you work out your own schedules and timetables for assignments and other work? Do you use a chart or other type of notes? Check if you do something similar to other learners.*

Exercise 2

▶ **3.2** Explain the situation and ask students to read the questions. Play the listening. Students compare answers in pairs and then do whole-class feedback.

Answers
1 To get an update on the project and check all the deadlines so far.
2 Stages 1, 2, 4 and 5
3 Week 4. Evidence from the audio script: '[Marketing and IT] have had three weeks to decide [in equipment costings]' (= end of week 3 / beginning of week 4); 'I've already received [the feedback] … everyone replied before the deadline [of week 4]' (=beginning of week 4)

Exercise 3

▶ **3.2** Ask students to read the sentences. Play the listening again. Students compare answers in pairs and then do whole-class feedback.

Answers
1 've agreed
2 Did you place
3 Has anyone given
4 replied

Exercise 4

Refer students to the *Tip*. Ask them to read the answers in **3** and do a and b in the *Language point*. Then ask them to read sentences 1–3 and complete the explanations with the adverbs in bold in the example sentences. Get feedback on answers with the whole class, eliciting why students' answers are not correct if they choose the wrong option.

Answers
a 1, 3
b 2, 4
1 just
2 yet
3 already

Grammar reference

If students need more information, go to *Grammar reference* on page 111 of the *Student's Book*.

Exercise 5

▶ **3.3** Ask students to read the conversation and decide which verb form to use and which adverb is correct. Tell students to look at the chart in **1** to remind them of the stages and dates on the project management chart. Play the listening once for students to check their answers. When students have compared answers in pairs, do whole-class feedback, eliciting why students' answers are not correct if they choose the wrong option.

Answers
1 Has, arrived
2 yet
3 just
4 left
5 Did, deliver
6 've unpacked
7 already

Further practice

If students need more practice, go to *Practice file 3* on page 111 of the *Student's Book*.

Exercise 6

Students work in pairs and ask and answer questions about this schedule for an office relocation project. They should use the past simple, present perfect and adverbs (*already, just, yet*) in their questions and answers.

EXTENSION Change pairs and ask students to change the 'Done?' column so different things are done or not done, and give different 'Additional information'. Then students do the exercise again.

Exercise 7

Students work in pairs and tell each other about a particular project they are working on, explaining each stage and what has already been done or hasn't been done yet.

PRE-WORK LEARNERS Ask students to imagine they are working on a particular project for a (real) well-known company. Give them time to think about the different stages and what has or hasn't been done.

DICTIONARY SKILLS
Check students understand what a collocation is: a group of words that frequently appear together. Learning vocabulary as collocations helps students express ideas more accurately.

Write the phrases *meet the deadline, fall behind schedule, get on with a task* on the board and ask students to check in their dictionaries which other words go with the nouns: *deadline, schedule, task* to form common verb + noun collocations. The answers will vary according to the dictionary they use, but the following are common collocations:
miss the deadline, work to a deadline, set a deadline, extend a deadline
have a schedule, stick to a schedule, work to a schedule
complete a task, set a task, carry out a task, give someone a task
Remind students that they should always record collocations as expressions and not as single words.

Photocopiable worksheet

Download and photocopy *Unit 3 Language at work worksheet* from the teacher resources in the *Online practice*.

Practically speaking

Exercise 1

Start by asking students questions and telling them they can only give you short answers, for example, *Did you send the email yesterday? Yes, I did. Have you finished working out the costings? No, I haven't.* Tell students to read the *Tip* and remind them we don't normally answer Yes/No questions with one-word answers, as it sounds rude or abrupt, and tends to stop the flow of the conversation. We generally add an auxiliary verb or short expression. Ask students to match the questions to the short answers.

Answers
1 d 2 a 3 c 4 b

Exercise 2

▶ **3.4** Explain that students are going to listen to the questions and answers with sentences which carry on the conversation. Ask the students to add the sentences to the short answers in **1**. Play the listening and let students compare answers in pairs before checking answers with the whole class.

EXTENSION Ask students to practise the conversations, focusing on the intonation. Monitor and correct intonation as necessary.

Exercise 3

Ask students to decide what each of the extra sentences in **2** is adding to the answers.

Answers
a 3 b 4 c 1 d 2

PRONUNCIATION When we use auxiliary verbs in questions, we use the weak form. In short answers, we use the strong form.

have
Have you checked the dates on the chart? /(h)əv/ (weak)
Yes, I have. I checked it yesterday before the meeting. / hæv/ (strong)

Other common auxiliary verbs that have weak and strong forms are: *am, are, do, does, has, can.*

Ask students to ask each other questions, and answer, using strong and weak forms.

Exercise 4

Give students time to write three questions individually. Ask students to work with a partner, taking turns to ask and answer the questions. They answer with short answers and add more information, for example, making a promise or giving an update.

Monitor and make sure the students respond using the target expressions in **1** and **2** and with the correct pronunciation.

Business communication

Exercise 1

Discuss the questions briefly with the whole class.

PRE-WORK LEARNERS Ask students how often they have to attend academic meetings. What is discussed in these meetings? How important are the meetings for the students? Do they attend meetings for sports clubs or teams? What happens at these meetings?

Exercise 2

▶ **3.5** Ask students to look at the notes and think about the information they need to listen for. Make sure students understand *recruit, recruitment* and *induction*. Remind students that these are Ramon's notes, so the answers are from his point of view, and not simply exactly what they hear. Play the listening. Let students compare answers in pairs and then check with the whole class.

Answers
2 next week
3 someone to help her do the interviews
4 do the interviews with Sue
6 the week after next
7 Sue (and Ramon) away on holiday + Eloise can't do it
8 Derek to do the induction training

Exercise 3

▶ **3.5** Ask students to look at the expressions before they listen. Play the listening again. Students number the expressions and compare answers in pairs. If necessary, play the listening again and pause after each sentence to elicit the answer.

Answers
8 Sorry, but I've never run induction training before.
11 Eloise is going to interview with Sue.
2 Is that something you can help with?
10 Let's check we all know what we're doing.
5 What's happening with that?
7 Can anyone else help you?
4 I'd like you to help if possible.
9 Would you like to help with that?
3 Yes, no problem.
6 I'd do it, but I'm away as well that week.

Exercise 4

Students work in groups of three. They are having a meeting to organize a visit to their company from ten business students on the 23rd of the month. They need to organize three tasks, following the flow chart. Refer students to the *Key expressions* to help them carry out the tasks. Student A is running the meeting. When they have completed the three tasks, Student A sums up the action plan, making sure Students B and C know exactly what they have to do.

ONE-TO-ONE Have the meeting with the student to discuss the visit using the prompts below. The teacher can take the role of either A or B:

A Give an update of the time and place of the students' visit and ask B to book a room for the talk (task 1).

B Agree to do task 1 and ask A to get the name badges (task 2).

A Say you can't do task 2 and give a reason. Ask B to do it.

B Agree to do task 2 and ask A to organize the refreshments (task 3).

A Agree to do task 3. Sum up the action plan.

Swap roles and repeat.

Exercise 5

Students practise in pairs. Student A turns to page 137, and B to page 142. Set the activity up either as a phone call or a meeting. Tell students to do the task as instructed. Monitor and make sure the students are clear on what tasks they have to do at the end of the exercise and that they are using the language from the *Key expressions*.

ONE-TO-ONE Make sure the student gets to ask some of the questions and not just play a passive role in the conversation. You could sit back to back with the student if you choose a phone call, so he/she really has to concentrate on listening to the instructions.

Photocopiable worksheet

Download and photocopy *Unit 3 Business communication worksheet* from the teacher resources in the *Online practice*.

Talking point

Discussion

Check students understand what scenario planning is. If they don't, ask them some *What if …?* questions, for example, *What if you miss your bus/train home? What if your car breaks down on the way home?* They can then come up with suggestions for what they might do. Tell students to read the information on Scenario planning and answer these questions: *Why does a huge multinational company like Royal Dutch Shell have a Plan B? How can a company develop its Plan B?*

Exercise 1

Ask students to discuss the question with a partner.

> **Possible answer**
> It is very important because the company has considered several possible outcomes and can react accordingly. It is therefore more flexible and there are fewer unforeseen problems.

Exercise 2

Ask students to think about a plan and think of three or four things that could go wrong in short and long-term planning.

> **Possible answers**
> strategic: financial situation of the company changes, government regulations change, new technology makes their technology obsolete
> operational: missing deadlines, people involved do not complete the jobs on time, materials may not arrive at the right time or in the right place for each stage

Exercise 3

Ask students to discuss the questions in small groups.

PRE-WORK LEARNERS Ask students to imagine they are working for a (real) well-known company. Give them time to think about the different stages in a project and what may not have been completed as scheduled.

Task

Exercise 1

Students work in groups. Ask them to decide what sort of company they work for. They have to prepare a Plan A and then a Plan B for a special day of events to celebrate an anniversary. Tell them to decide on the details for the event, for example, *What is the special anniversary? What events are appropriate for the company and this anniversary? Who will come to the celebration? Are there any formal events? If so, what are they and who is involved?*

PRE-WORK LEARNERS Ask students to imagine that their university/college is having a special anniversary, for example it was founded 100 years ago. Ask them to prepare a Plan A and Plan B for a special day of celebrations.

Exercise 2

The group makes notes on the Plan A, making a basic schedule/chart for the stages of the plan.

Exercise 3

Once Plan A is clear and there is a schedule, then the group starts scenario planning, asking *What if …?* for each of the stages and coming up with an alternative to make sure the event runs smoothly.

Exercise 4

The group then organizes a presentation of the Plan A, including the Plan B scenarios, to the rest of the class. All of the group should take part in the presentation, so each member presents a section of the plans. The group should be prepared to answer questions on its plans and scenarios.

The class listens and asks questions at the end of each presentation. At the end of the presentations, the class can decide which scenarios they think will work best.

ONE-TO-ONE The student plans the presentation and gives it to you. You ask questions to check he/she has thought of various scenarios, and their solutions. You should then ask some *What if …?* questions to give him/her more practice. For example, *What if the … stage is running late? What effect will this have? Can you think of any ideas on how to get it back on track again?*

Progress test

Download and photocopy *Unit 3 Progress test* and *Speaking test* from the teacher resources in the *Online practice*.

Viewpoint 1

Preview

The topic of this *Viewpoint* is *Sharing a workspace*. In this *Viewpoint*, students begin by watching and discussing a video of three people talking about things they share with other people in their work, for example, shared desks, printers, etc. Students then watch and discuss a video about the HUB – a shared workspace in Islington, London. Finally, the students do a task which involves deciding whether the HUB would be a good place to work.

Exercise 1

Allow students time to look at the list. Check they understand the meaning of *sharing* in this context (you could use 'hot-desking' as an example). Then ask students to discuss the list with a partner.

PRE-WORK LEARNERS Ask students to think about their college or university. Ask them to tell their partner which of these facilities they share with other people. Don't let them discuss how they feel about it yet, as that comes up later.

- transport to and from college/university
- classrooms
- a library
- desks
- photocopying and stationery
- computer access
- the course
- anything else?

Exercise 2

▶ 01 Make sure the students look at the questions in the table to check exactly what they are listening for before watching the video. Play the video and ask students to take notes. If necessary, pause after each speaker to allow writing time.

Answers

	What do they share?	Are there any advantages or disadvantages?
Speaker 1	Office, laptop, printer, kitchen	+ Nice to be with other people – Everybody has different idea of comfort
Speaker 2	Tools	+ Cost and space, respect
Speaker 3	(office) Space	+ Colleagues know what you are working on, so helps decision making and problem solving – Can be extremely distracting

EXTRA ACTIVITY You could spend some time here on helping students take notes efficiently. Firstly, ask students to read the questions carefully and decide which words are the key words, and what information they should listen for: *What/share? Advantages/disadvantages?*

Then tell them not to try to write down every word but to listen for key words in the answers. Explain how to recognize these – key words are usually a little longer, louder and even have higher intonation, as they are the stressed words. Give students one or two sentences as examples:

I work in an open-plan office. I share my desk with two people.

Remind them that sometimes they will not hear the exact words from the questions in the answers; the person answering the question may use synonyms, or paraphrase the question, for example:

An advantage is that we work in an open-plan office. = One good thing is that where we work is light and airy.

Exercise 3

Ask the students to discuss the questions in pairs. You could have whole-class feedback by asking one or two pairs for their ideas.

Exercise 4

Ask students to look at the pictures of the HUB and discuss with a partner what they think is happening. *Where could the people be? What could they be doing?* Have the students ever experienced working or studying in a similar situation? Ask them if they know what *hub* means (the central and most important part of a particular place or activity). You could draw a wheel with a hub and spokes to show them where the word *hub* comes from.

Tell students they are going to watch a video about sharing a workspace and that the words and phrases in **4** are from the video. Tell them to work with a partner and match the words and phrases 1–7 to the definitions a–g. Check answers as a whole class.

Answers
1 c **2** g **3** e **4** a **5** b **6** f **7** d

PRONUNCIATION Check pronunciation of phrases 1–7 with students. Ask them to mark the word stress and practise saying them with a partner.

Answers
di<u>ve</u>rse <u>back</u>ground, <u>sec</u>tors, cam<u>paign</u>ers go <u>cra</u>zy with <u>lone</u>liness, per<u>spec</u>tive, re<u>sourc</u>es, a <u>glob</u>al <u>net</u>work

Exercise 5

▶ 02 Tell students to read A–E carefully and decide what key words they are listening for, for example *location = place where, it's in …*, etc. Then play the video, telling students to number A–E in the correct order 1–5. Students compare answers with a partner. Then check answers as a whole class.

Answers
A 1 B 5 C 4 D 3 E 2

VIDEO SCRIPT

This building is the HUB. It's in Islington, in north London. The HUB is a work-space for lots of different people. Most people at the HUB are self-employed with small businesses.

Some people also work for the HUB. Anna Levy has worked here for about three years. She's a host and she's responsible for helping the people who use the HUB.

What sort of people use the HUB?
There's all sorts, people from very, very diverse backgrounds, different kinds of, of skills and experience and sectors. So, from media, we have web design, consultants of various sorts, and campaigners – people from lots of different backgrounds.

Lots of people come to the HUB because they don't want to work from home. It's a good place for meeting other people and sharing information and ideas. They can also share office equipment which is expensive to buy.

Do you think working at the HUB is better than working from home?
It's a million times better than working from home. For a start, it's a lot more sociable, so a lot of people that come to The HUB have been working at home for maybe one or two years, and they're going crazy with loneliness, and they have nobody to share ideas with. And so, just from the perspective, from the social perspective, it's, it's a lot better.

What office equipment can users of the HUB share?
They also have access to, to resources that you, you wouldn't have at home, so, like a printer and things like that, and scanner, and mailbox, and the sort of thing that you need when you start a business, and the sort of thing that you're used to having in a traditional office.

The HUB in Islington is very popular, and there are four more HUBs in London. The idea of the HUB is also growing around the world. At the moment, there are over 30 HUBs on five continents, with over 5,000 members. It's a global network of individual people who enjoy working together, and who can see the advantages of sharing a work-space, different ideas and experiences with others.

Exercise 6

Students work with a partner. Ask them to read the sentences and decide if they are true or false. Ask them to give reasons for their answers and, if they can remember, to give the true answers to the false sentences.

Exercise 7

▶ 02 Play the video again for students to check their answers, making sure they listen closely and write down the relevant words and phrases. Stop the video and check the words and phrases used where relevant.

Answers
1 F (Most people at the HUB are self-employed with small businesses.)
2 T (Anna Levy has worked here for about three years.)
3 F (There's all sorts, people from very, very diverse backgrounds, different kinds of skills and experience and sectors.)
4 T (It's a good place for meeting other people and sharing information and ideas. / It's a lot more sociable.)
5 T (They also have access to, to resources that you, you wouldn't have at home.)
6 F (The HUB in Islington is very popular, and there are four more HUBs in London. The idea of the HUB is also growing around the world. At the moment, there are over 30 HUBs in five continents.)
7 T (At the moment, there are over 30 HUBs in five continents, with over 5,000 members.)

Exercise 8

Ask students to discuss the question in small groups. Tell them to look at the picture and describe how they might feel about working there.

Exercise 9

Students work with a partner. Ask them to read the instructions for either Student A or Student B and prepare what they are going to say.

ONE-TO-ONE Tell the student that his/her company is looking into the possibility of having a shared workspace in the main office. Ask him/her to prepare a presentation to you, as the CEO, on the reasons for adopting this style of working or not, what advantages it could have for the company, and what disadvantages there might be. He/she should also be prepared to answer some questions from the CEO.

When he/she has given the presentation, have four or five questions to ask. After the presentation and questions, ask him/her to decide how useful/relevant this sort of shared workspace would be for his/her actual company.

Exercise 10

In their pairs, Students A and B have the conversation. When they have finished, they can decide whether they think the HUB is a good place for Student B to work and give their reasons.

Exercise 11

Students change partners and swap roles and repeat the conversation, deciding whether the HUB is a good place for Student A to work and giving their reasons.

Give whole-class feedback by checking what each group came up with. You could have a vote to see what the class thinks of sharing workspace as a whole.

Further video ideas

You can find a list of suggested ideas for how to use video in the class in the teacher resources in the *Online practice*.

By the end of this unit, students will be able to
- talk about services and systems
- make comparisons
- talk about approximate numbers
- talk about features and benefits.

Context

The topic of *Services & systems* gives students the language to describe the technical services and systems within a company. A successful twenty-first century company cannot afford to fall behind in technology and must keep up with the latest developments. It is not only essential to keep up with developments, but also to be able to evaluate new systems and services and decide on their relevance to the company. To do this, students cover the language needed to compare and contrast what they are evaluating.

It is important to be able to use approximate numbers when evaluating. Students will describe graphs and tables using approximation expressions. They will also describe particular features and assess their benefits.

In this unit, students will learn how to describe technical services and systems, assessing the main benefits to their company and their own workload. They will have the opportunity to practise discussing and questioning the benefits of new systems.

In the *Talking point*, the students will discuss a staff evaluation system and stack ranking, and role-play a meeting between managers and employees, discussing the system and proposing ways to improve employee performance. They will present the outcome of the meeting.

Starting point

Do the first question with the whole class. Give them cues if they are hesitant: *How do you usually get cash, pay bills, buy things, etc.? Where do you keep your work on your computer? How do you get your news?* The second and third questions can be done with the whole class or in pairs before whole-class feedback. Encourage students to develop their answers.

PRE-WORK LEARNERS   Ask students to discuss these prompts for question 3 in small groups and then report back to the class. *Do you have any experience of using online services? Which companies do you think give a good service? Do you have any experience of poor service? If so, give an example.*

Working with words

Exercise 1

Allow students a few minutes to think about the apps they have on various devices, mobile phones, tablets, laptops, etc. Ask students to discuss, in pairs, how they use them and compare their ideas. Ask one or two pairs to share their ideas in whole-class feedback.

Exercise 2

Ask students to read the questions and then the reviews. Tell students it's not necessary to understand all the words, only the general sense. Provide feedback on answers with the whole class.

Answers		
	a	b
App 1	can book a taxi, reduces waiting time, uses GPS to find a driver, it's safe, no cash is involved	perhaps a person who travels a lot and needs to get round cities quickly
App 2	easier for scheduling meetings with lots of people, no excuses for being late	people who have lots of meetings with people in different departments
App 3	keeps track of investments, follows any stock market, provides clear infographics	investors on the move

Exercise 3

Ask students to compare answers to the questions in small groups. If students don't use apps like these, ask them to think of specific situations where they could be useful, or to think of apps that would be useful to them. After the group work, provide feedback with the whole class.

Exercise 4

You could check the first answer with the whole class and then ask students to complete the other answers individually. Let them compare answers with a partner before doing whole-class feedback.

Answers
1 user-friendly
2 accurate
3 secure
4 high-quality
5 handy
6 up-to-date
7 efficient

PRONUNCIATION Ask students to mark the stress on the words from **4**. Students can then practise in pairs by covering the answers in **4**. Student A gives Student B the opposite adjective, and Student B answers with the correct adjective. They then swap roles.

Monitor, checking students are stressing the right syllables.

Answers
user-<u>friend</u>ly
<u>ac</u>curate
se<u>cure</u>
high-<u>qual</u>ity
<u>han</u>dy
up-to-<u>date</u>
ef<u>fic</u>ient

ONE-TO-ONE You read the opposite adjectives for the student to practise.

Exercise 5

You could check the first answer with the whole class and then ask them to complete the other sentences individually. Let them compare answers with a partner before doing whole-class feedback.

Answers
1 efficient
2 up-to-date
3 secure
4 user-friendly
5 time-consuming
6 difficult to use
7 accurate

Exercise 6

Ask students to work in pairs and use the adjectives in **4** to describe the services and systems. Check the answers in whole-class feedback. Ask students to give real life examples if they can.

Possible answers
Online banking: secure, user-friendly, up-to-date
System for booking a meeting room at work: efficient/time-consuming
Passport control at an airport: time-consuming/efficient
A child care service for working parents: handy, secure

Exercise 7

▶ 4.1 Tell students they are going to listen to three people talking about a service or system from **6**. Ask them to read the questions in the table and decide what information they should listen for. Tell them to make notes. Play the listening. Let them compare answers with a partner, then get feedback from the whole class.

Answers

	Speaker 1	Speaker 2	Speaker 3
1	System for booking a meeting room	Passport control	Childcare services
2	Yes, because it's quite well-designed though it isn't always accurate.	No, because the machine wouldn't recognize the passport.	Yes, because it's friendly and secure and allows you to keep working full-time.

Exercise 8

Refer students to the *Tip*. Let students read the sentences and decide which verbs are correct. They can then compare their answers with another pair's and decide on the sentences where both verbs are possible. Check answers with the whole class.

Answers
1 makes it easier
2 lets
3 allows
4 lets / helps
5 enables / allows

Further practice

If students need more practice, go to *Practice file 4* on page 112 of the *Student's Book*.

Exercise 9

Students work individually initially, making notes on three more services and systems that make their working or personal lives easier. Then they take turns to describe their services and systems to a partner. You could ask students to decide which two services or systems they think are the most effective.

PRE-WORK LEARNERS Ask students to think about three more services and systems which would make their school or college life and/or personal life easier. They can compare ideas with two or three other students, and then come up with a list of the three best services and systems to make their college life and/or personal life easier.

EXTENSION Ask each student to prepare a 30-second presentation on one of their services or systems to the class. In that time, they have to convince everyone to make use of it. The class can vote on whether they would use it.

Photocopiable worksheet

Download and photocopy *Unit 4 Working with words worksheet* from the teacher resources in the *Online practice*.

Language at work

Exercise 1

Ask students to discuss the questions in pairs. Ask one or two pairs to give feedback to the whole class.

PRE-WORK LEARNERS Ask students about the online services they use for studying. What types of software programmes do they use for their studies and for their personal things?

What other online systems do they use regularly? Which do they find most useful?

Exercise 2

Explain the situation and ask students to read the sentences. Ask students to complete the sentences and then compare answers in pairs. Then do whole-class feedback.

Answers
1 more accurate
2 longer
3 easier
4 less time-consuming
5 user-friendly

Exercise 3

Ask students to read the sentences in **2** again. They then complete the *Language point*. Students compare answers in pairs and then do whole-class feedback.

Answers
1 far, a lot
2 a little, slightly
3 almost

Grammar reference

If students need more information, go to *Grammar reference* on page 113 of the *Student's Book*.

Exercise 4

▶ **4.2** Tell students they are going to listen to part of a phone conversation between an after-sales representative from Ercho and a user of their software.

Ask students to read the information in the table to check what they are listening for. Let students compare answers with a partner.

Give feedback on answers with the whole class, eliciting why students' answers are not correct if they chose the wrong option.

Answers

User feedback on	Better?	Big difference?	Comments?
the new version of the software	Y	Yes	It works a lot more efficiently.
using the customer-profile system	Y	No. A little.	You could find a profile almost as easily on the old version.
filling in the order forms	N	Small difference	Staff are filling it in a little more slowly.

Exercise 5

▶ **4.2** Play the listening. Ask students to read the sentences and fill in the missing words. Students check answers with a partner, before whole-class feedback.

Answers
1 better
2 more efficiently
3 easily
4 useful
5 more slowly

Exercise 6

Elicit quickly the difference between an adjective and an adverb. If necessary, give an example of each: *It is easier to use the new system.* (adj.) *You can find the information more easily.* (adv.) Refer students to the *Tip*. Students work in pairs. Check with whole-class feedback, eliciting why answers are not correct, if necessary.

Answers
Adjectives: better
Adverbs: more efficiently, almost as easily, more slowly, more useful

EXTENSION Dictate some adjectives to the class, for example, *good, correct, safe, useful, efficient, accurate, secure, hard, quiet*. Ask students to write the adverb form of each one. Then ask the students to work in pairs, choose five of the adverbs and write a comparative sentence for each. They then take turns to read out their sentence to another pair, leaving out the comparative adverb. The other pair has to decide what the missing comparative forms are.

Further practice

If students need more practice, go to *Practice file 4* on page 113 of the *Student's Book*.

Exercise 7

Students work in pairs and use the information in the table to make sentences comparing two financial software products. Monitor, checking students are using the correct comparative form and modifier. Ask two or three pairs for sentences in the whole-class feedback.

Possible answers
2 Staff can learn to use Accounter 3.1 a little more easily than Financepro.
3 Financepro is almost as secure as Accounter 3.1.
4 Technical support with Accounter 3.1 can help much more quickly.
5 Accounter 3.1 is far more up-to-date than Financepro.

EXTENSION With stronger students, the pair work in **7** can become a role-play. Student A is a telemarketer who calls potential customers. Student A calls Student B and tries to convince him/her to sign up for A's chosen service. Student A needs to describe what it will make easier, and Student B suggests drawbacks or reasons not to buy this service.

Exercise 8

Students make a similar table about one of their company's products or services, comparing it to their main competitor's. In pairs, they make sentences about it. If all the students work in the same company, ask them to find information on the Internet about another company's product and make a similar table to make sentences.

PRE-WORK LEARNERS Tell students to imagine they work for a (real) well-known company. Students work in pairs, each for a different company. Each student finds information on the Internet about a product or service of the company they choose and make a similar table to make sentences.

Photocopiable worksheet

Download and photocopy *Unit 4 Language at work worksheet* from the teacher resources in the *Online practice*.

Practically speaking

Exercise 1

If your students work, start by asking them about the management software used in their company. *Is it easy to use? Is it often updated? What happens when there's an update?* Ask students to look at the information in the graph and answer the questions.

> **Answers**
> 130 people responded to the question.
> Most companies install new software using an in-house person.

Exercise 2

▶ 4.3 Explain that students are going to listen to someone describing the results in the table. Refer the students to the *Tip*. Before they listen, ask them to think of words they might use to approximate numbers, *around, up to,* etc. Play the listening and let students compare answers in pairs before checking answers with the whole class.

> **Answers**
> 130: well over one hundred
> 31%: nearly a third
> 54.5%: about half
> 14.5%: a little under 15%

Exercise 3

Ask students to match the synonyms. Then they compare with a partner.

> **Answers**
> 1 d   2 a   3 b   4 c

Exercise 4

Write some expressions on the board, for example, *34%, 292, 2003, 23%,* and ask students to say what they are, using approximate numbers, *well over thirty per cent, just below three hundred, around two thousand, almost a quarter.* Students take turns to describe the numbers in the exercise in pairs. Check that they use the correct stress in each expression.

> **Possible answers**
> 1,002: just over a thousand / around a thousand
> 37%: about a third / just over a third
> 240: well over two hundred / just below two hundred and fifty
> 49%: almost half / almost a half / around half
> 67%: around two thirds / just over two thirds

Exercise 5

Students work in pairs. If all the students work in the same company, ask them to find information on the Internet relating to the prompts about another company and, if they want, a different country.

PRE-WORK LEARNERS Tell students to imagine they work for a (real) well-known company in a different country. Students work in pairs, each for a different company. Each student finds information on the Internet about the company they work for and describes the company and country using the prompts.

Business communication

Exercise 1

Ask the students to read the information and answer the questions.

> **Answers**
> 1 Employees might feel that the software is controlling them and watching their working lives.
> 2 The company could argue that the software enables payroll to be accurate and that it offers employees flexible working.

Exercise 2

▶ 4.4 Ask students to look at the headings and think about the information they need to listen for. Play the listening. Let students compare answers in pairs. Then check with the whole class.

> **Answers**
> 1 Accurate payroll feature, you can log on and off manually or automatically, the phone app lets you log on when overseas. It's easier for managers as there will be fewer mistakes as no forms to fill in.
> 2 Forgetting to log on in the morning, not getting paid, adjusting settings on the computer, logging on overseas, will the manager know if I'm working?

Exercise 3

▶ 4.4 Ask students to look at the expressions and match them before they listen. Play the listening again, students check the answers. If necessary, listen again and pause after each sentence to elicit the answer.

> **Answers**
> 1 c   2 b   3 f   4 i   5 h   6 d   7 g   8 a   9 e   10 j

PRONUNCIATION Sometimes students find long sentences difficult to repeat. Explain how they are 'chunked' into groups of words that go together in sense groups when we speak. Ask them to mark where they think the sense groups of words are. Then ask them to mark the stressed word in each chunk. They then practise saying the sentences.

> **Answers**
> 1 The <u>main</u> benefit is // the <u>payroll</u> feature.
> 2 It's a <u>lot</u> more accurate // because it auto<u>mat</u>ically knows // how many <u>hours</u> // you've <u>worked</u> each month.
> 3 <u>One</u> of the problems // is that your <u>man</u>ager // has to fill in a <u>form</u> // for <u>each</u> of you.
> 4 What <u>happens</u> // if I forget to <u>log on</u> // in the <u>morning</u> // <u>when</u> I start work?
> 5 <u>That</u>'s a good <u>question</u>.
> 6 But wouldn't that re<u>quire</u> us // to have to ad<u>just</u> // the <u>settings</u> on our com<u>pu</u>ters?
> 7 It might <u>seem</u> // that you'd <u>need</u> to adjust your settings, // but in <u>fact</u> // the <u>soft</u>ware can do this auto<u>mat</u>ically.
> 8 Will it let me <u>log on</u> // from a ho<u>tel</u>?
> 9 I'm <u>not</u> convinced // that it's <u>poss</u>ible to do that // <u>every</u> time you're abroad.
> 10 I'm <u>sure</u> you'll find it // <u>much</u> easier to use // than the <u>current</u> system.

Further practice

If students need more practice, go to *Practice file 4* on page 112 of the *Student's Book*.

Exercise 4

Students work in pairs. They read the information about a new computer system and make two lists. Refer students to the *Key expressions*. Then ask the pairs to present their lists to the whole class.

> **Suggested answers**
> 1 Benefits: improve employee performance, monthly performance appraisals, bonuses for excellent performance, 'employee of the month' award.
> 2 Possible problems: makes employees compete against each other, how will managers judge performance? Time-consuming to meet your manager at the end of every month.

Exercise 5

Students practise in the same pairs. Student A turns to page 138, and B to page 142. Using the information from the lists they made in **4**, tell students to follow the instructions. Refer students to the *Key expressions* to help them carry out the task. Monitor and make sure the students are clear on what tasks they have to do and that they are using the expressions correctly.

ONE-TO-ONE Start with the student playing Student A and then swap roles, so he/she gets a chance to cover all the language.

Photocopiable worksheet

Download and photocopy *Unit 4 Business communication worksheet* from the teacher resources in the *Online practice*.

Talking point

Discussion

Exercise 1

Check students understand the idea of *assessing* and *ranking*. Ask them if they have been ranked at work, or how they would feel if they were. Ask students to read the article and discuss the questions in small groups.

> **Possible answer**
> It's controversial because even if the lowest 10% work hard, they are still ranked as 'poor'.

Exercise 2

Ask students to discuss the questions in the same groups and then check in whole-class feedback.

> **Possible answers**
> It's an easy way for managers to measure employee performance. You could work out who gets pay increases and who doesn't using this ranking. It creates competition and may demotivate many employees. It also allows for manager bias.

Exercise 3

Ask students to discuss the question in their groups, then one person from each group can sum up what they decided and why, for the rest of the class.

Task

Exercise 1

Students work in groups of four. Set up the situation and ask them to divide into pairs of managers and employees.

Exercise 2

Give students time to prepare their arguments and make lists of possible changes. Remind them that they will present their arguments and the decisions they agree on to the class.

Exercise 3

Start the meeting. It might be a good idea to give the groups a time limit to present their arguments and discuss possible changes. A few minutes before the end of the task, ask the groups to reach an agreement.

Exercise 4

Each group then presents their changes to the class. Those listening can ask questions.

ONE-TO-ONE Do the task with the student as manager, then swap roles. Ask him/her to present the changes at the end.

Progress test

Download and photocopy *Unit 4 Progress test* and *Speaking test* from the teacher resources in the *Online practice*.

Unit content

By the end of this unit, students will be able to

- talk about customer service
- talk about schedules and future arrangements using present tenses
- say 'sorry' in different ways
- make and change arrangements.

Context

The topic of *Customers* gives students the language to talk about, and to, customers and clients. Every company has to take good care of its customers and give good service in order to encourage customer loyalty. This is also true of online companies. It is essential for companies to meet customers' expectations, and ensure customers are satisfied by making good customer care a priority. To do this, students cover the language needed for the essential aspects of customer care.

It is important to be able to talk about schedules, events and arrangements. Students will learn to use the present simple and present continuous to talk about scheduled events and make arrangements.

Social interaction between colleagues is crucial for effective teamwork in both formal and informal situations. Cultural differences can lead to misunderstandings if colleagues do not use the appropriate expressions for apologizing and explaining the situation.

In this unit, students will learn how to make and, where necessary, change arrangements. They will have the opportunity to practise setting up and rearranging appointments.

In the *Talking point*, students will have the opportunity to discuss a variation in management styles, including upside down management, and role-play a discussion where the benefits and drawbacks of this style of management are assessed. They then decide whether the company should introduce the system and present the outcome of the meeting.

Starting point

Do the first question with the whole class. Give them cues if they are hesitant: *Who do you normally have contact with at work? Who do you visit regularly? Who do you phone/email?* The second and third questions can be done with the whole class or in pairs before whole-class feedback. Encourage students to develop their answers.

PRE-WORK LEARNERS Ask students to think about their own college or university. Do they feel as if they are customers there? Why/Why not? How do they feel as customers there?

Working with words

Exercise 1

Allow students a few minutes to think about and discuss the quote. How true do they think it is for their type of business? It might be useful to check they know who Jeff Bezos is (the founder and Chief Executive Officer of Amazon.com), how successful Amazon is, and why it might be a good idea to listen to him. You could ask them to find out from the Internet. Ask one or two pairs to share the ideas they came up with in whole-class feedback.

PRE-WORK LEARNERS Ask students to think about how they find out about products and services. Do they speak to people they know or do they read about the product/service online? How important are online ratings when they are making their decisions? Ask them to give an example.

Exercise 2

Ask students to read the article and the titles and choose the best one. Tell students it's not necessary to understand all the words, only the general sense. Provide whole-class feedback.

Suggested answer
b Delivering happiness

Exercise 3

Ask students to look at the numbers and then scan the article to find them in the text. Then in pairs they discuss what the numbers refer to. You could explain about scanning here. Remind them that when we scan a text we are looking for specific pieces of information, for example, information about a number or a date. Tell students not to read every word, but to move quickly through the article and stop when they come to the information they want. Then they read the sentence with the number or date carefully and note the relevant information. Ask students which texts we generally scan, for example, timetables, dictionaries, online research, etc.

Answers
5,000 calls answered per day
1,200 emails answered per week
4 weeks' staff training in how to make customers happy
10 hours and 29 minutes: the longest customer care phone call ever
75% repeat orders

Exercise 4

Students underline the words that are true for them and add a reason. Let them compare answers with a partner before doing whole-class feedback.

PRE-WORK LEARNERS Ask students to discuss sentence prompt 2, thinking about a company they regularly have to deal with.

Exercise 5

Ask students to complete the table. Show them where the first answer is, if necessary. Let them compare answers with a partner before doing whole-class feedback.

Answers

2	loyalty	6	satisfaction
3	expectation	7	production
4	required	8	to deliver
5	service		

DICTIONARY SKILLS
Write *satisfactory, satisfied, satisfying* on the board and ask students to check their meanings in their dictionary. Then ask students to write three sentences with the words in.

Exercise 6

Ask students to work in pairs to try to complete the paragraph with the correct form of the words. Do whole-class feedback.

Answers

1	expect	5	service(s)
2	deliver	6	cares
3	satisfied	7	loyal
4	expectations		

Exercise 7

Students work in pairs. Tell them to scan the text in **2** again and find the word *customer*. Ask them to complete the mind map with any collocations with *customer* they find. You could draw the map on the board to check answers in whole-class feedback.

Answers
customer complaints, customer loyalty, customer expectations, customer service, customer satisfaction

Exercise 8

Refer students to the *Tip*. Students work in pairs to complete the sentences with a collocation from **7**. Check the answers in whole-class feedback.

Answers
1 service/care/satisfaction/loyalty
2 loyalty
3 complaints
4 satisfaction/loyalty

DICTIONARY SKILLS
Write *customer* and *client* on the board. Ask students to divide into two groups, A and B. Ask them to decide what the difference is between a customer and a client. Then ask Group A to find at least six words that collocate with *customer*, and Group B to find six that collocate with *client*. Then divide the class into pairs, Student A and Student B. A teaches B his/her six collocations, and B teaches A his/her six.

Possible collocations
customer: key customer, loyal customer, potential customer, customer dissatisfaction, customer profile, customer complaints, customer enquiries, deal with customers, attract customers
client: valued client, take on a client, serve clients, prospective client, regular client, corporate client, act for a client, on behalf of a client, attract clients

Exercise 9

Students work in pairs and take turns to ask and answer the questions in **8**. For whole-class feedback, ask different pairs to ask and answer the questions.

PRE-WORK LEARNERS Ask students to imagine they work for a company. They take turns asking and answering the questions. You could ask them to go to websites of (real) well-known companies to find the information.

Further practice
If students need more practice, go to *Practice file 5* on page 114 of the *Student's Book*.

Exercise 10

Students work in pairs to come up with five rules and guidelines for successful customer service. Remind them to add something extra to make each memorable, as in the example. For whole-class feedback, ask two or three pairs for their rules.

EXTENSION Ask pairs to join with another pair and compare rules and guidelines. Tell them to agree on a new set of five rules and guidelines for the group.

Then ask each group to present their rules and guidelines. After all the groups of four have presented their rules and guidelines, ask the class to decide on the best five rules and guidelines and write them on the board.

PRE-WORK LEARNERS Ask students to imagine they work for a (real) international online company and come up with the rules and guidelines. You could ask them to find information about online companies on the Internet before they start.

Photocopiable worksheet
Download and photocopy *Unit 5 Working with words worksheet* from the teacher resources in the *Online practice*.

Language at work

Exercise 1

Ask students to quickly make notes on any plans, meetings or events they know are going to happen this week, next week and next month. Working in pairs, they explain their schedule to their partner. Then they can talk about their busiest periods.

PRE-WORK LEARNERS Ask students to check their schedules and decide how busy they are this week. Then ask them to decide which time of the month/year is the busiest for them. What is it that makes this period so busy?

Exercise 2

Explain the situation and ask students to read the schedule and the email. Ask students to find what will change and then compare answers with a partner. Then do whole-class feedback.

Answers
Monday: Meeting at Aksa 17.00
Tuesday: Giray Demir is joining the customer visits.

Exercise 3

Ask students to read the email in **2** again quickly. With a partner, they decide what tenses the verbs in bold are and whether they refer to the present or to the future. Students then match the verbs in bold in the email to the explanations in the *Language point*.

Answers
The verbs actually refer to the future, although they are present forms.
1 leave, come back
2 're not meeting, aren't waiting, is joining
3 hope
4 are (busy), is (fine)

Grammar reference
If students need more information, go to *Grammar reference* on page 115 of the *Student's Book*.

Exercise 4

▶ **5.1** Ask students to quickly read the email in **2** again. Tell them they are going to listen to Anita's voicemail, where Giray makes additional changes. Students compare answers with a partner. Get feedback on answers with the whole class, eliciting why students' answers are not correct, if necessary.

Answers
Giray can't meet them personally at the airport on Monday evening. He will arrange a driver.
Giray will meet Anita and Hakan at the hotel reception at 8.30 because their first meeting is now at 9.30 instead of 11.00.

Exercise 5

▶ **5.1** Refer students to the *Tip*. Ask students to read the voicemail message and underline the correct form of the verbs. Students check answers with a partner. Play the listening. Give whole-class feedback and, if necessary, play the listening again, pausing at the answers to check.

Answers
1 'm	6 are you staying
2 arrives	7 'm not
3 to meet	8 are staying
4 are meeting	9 opens
5 to check	

EXTENSION Write ten verbs on the board, for example, *know, agree, get, live, remember, hate, listen, read, like, believe*. Ask students to decide which are state verbs and which are dynamic (action) verbs. Ask them to look at the verbs which describe thinking and liking things – are they generally state or dynamic verbs? Ask students to choose six verbs, three state and three dynamic verbs, and write sentences for them.

Exercise 6

Ask students to look at the schedule and make sentences with the prompts using present simple and present continuous for future events, plans and intentions. Let them compare answers with a partner. Check answers in whole-class feedback.

Possible answers
3 I'm not going to the first session. I'm too busy because I'm meeting clients.
4 I'm giving my presentation on Wednesday. It starts at 14.00 and finishes at 15.00.
5 I hope to go to the buffet reception on Wednesday evening.
6 I'm free on Thursday morning.
7 I plan to have lunch with Sally and Remi at 12.30.
8 I'm flying to Paris on Friday.
9 My flight leaves at 14.20 from Heathrow.

Further practice
If students need more practice, go to *Practice file 5* on page 115 of the *Student's Book*.

Exercise 7

Students work in pairs. Ask them to quickly write a schedule of events for next week. Ask students to compare schedules. Ask two or three pairs for sentences in whole-class feedback.

EXTENSION Tell students to arrange a meeting when they are both free. They can then tell the class when, where and why they are meeting.

Photocopiable worksheet
Download and photocopy *Unit 5 Language at work worksheet* from the teacher resources in the *Online practice*.

Practically speaking

Exercise 1

Start by asking students about a time they had to apologize at work. Why did they have to apologize? Who did they have to apologize to? Do they apologize in different ways to different people at work – a colleague they know well, a colleague they don't really know, the manager? They tell their partner about it. Ask one or two pairs to explain their situations to the whole class.

PRE-WORK LEARNERS Ask students to think about a situation where they had to say 'sorry'. Why did they apologize? Who did they have to apologize to? Do they apologize in different ways to different people – a friend, a classmate they don't know well, the teacher? They tell their partner about it. Ask one or two pairs to explain their situations to the whole class.

Exercise 2

▶ **5.2** Explain that students are going to listen to five people apologizing. Play the listening and ask them to match apologies 1–5 to the reasons a–e. Or you could ask them to match the apologies to the reasons first and then play the listening for them to check. Let students compare answers in pairs before checking answers with the whole class.

> **Answers**
> 2 e   3 a   4 c   5 d

Exercise 3

▶ **5.3** Ask students to match the responses a–e to the apologies 1–5 in **2**. Play the listening for students to listen and check.

> **Answers**
> **a** 2   **b** 5   **c** 3   **d** 4   **e** 1

PRONUNCIATION Tell students that to sound sincere they need to use rise and fall intonation when apologizing and explaining what happened. Say sentence 1, firstly with very flat intonation and then with polite intonation. Ask students if they can hear a difference. Write the sentence on the board and mark the correct intonation. Then play listening **5.3** again and ask students to take turns apologizing. Monitor, checking students are using the correct stress in the sentence.

> **Answers**
> 1 A I'm <u>sorry</u>, but I'm <u>busy</u> next Monday evening.
>   B No <u>problem</u>. How about <u>Tuesday</u> instead?
> 2 A I'm <u>sorry</u>, but can you re<u>peat</u> that?
>   B Sure. It's <u>A</u> as in <u>Al</u>pha.
> 3 A I'm <u>sorry</u> to keep you <u>wait</u>ing.
>   B <u>Not</u> to worry. We haven't <u>start</u>ed yet.
> 4 A I'm <u>sorry</u>, but the <u>traffic</u> was <u>terrible</u> this morning.
>   B That's OK. There was a <u>problem</u> with my <u>train</u> as well.
> 5 A I'm <u>sorry</u>, but can <u>I</u> say <u>some</u>thing at this point?
>   B Of <u>course</u>. Go a<u>head</u>.

Exercise 4

Students work in pairs. Ask them to take turns apologizing and responding. Monitor, correcting the pronunciation where necessary. Ask different pairs to apologize and respond for whole-class feedback.

PRE-WORK LEARNERS Tell students to take turns apologizing in four different situations: 1. Call the dentist's reception to explain you will be late for an appointment because of a train strike. 2. Tell your classmate that you can't attend his/her class presentation next week and give a good reason. 3. You made an arrangement to meet a friend after class, and you arrive 20 minutes late. 4. You didn't hear the teacher's explanation in the lesson. Apologize and ask him/her to repeat it.

Business communication

Exercise 1

Ask the students to read the information and answer the questions with a partner.

PRE-WORK LEARNERS Ask students to think about a well-known company and think about who the main suppliers could be, and what they are supplied with. You could ask them to find the information on the Internet as preparation.

Exercise 2

▶ **5.4** Ask students to look at the sentences and think about the information to listen for. Play the listening. Let students compare answers in pairs and then check with the whole class.

> **Answers**
> 1 B   2 E   3 S   4 E   5 B

Exercise 3

▶ **5.4** Ask students to read the expressions and try to say them in different ways using the prompts, before they listen. Play the listening again for students to check the answers. If necessary, play the listening again and pause after each sentence to elicit the answer.

> **Answers**
> 2 I'm afraid I'm always busy on Mondays.
> 3 I can't make it that day.
> 4 How about Tuesday?
> 5 That suits me.
> 6 Is two o'clock convenient?
> 7 Can we make it later?
> 8 So that's Tuesday the first at three.

Further practice

If students need more practice, go to *Practice file 5* on page 114 of the *Student's Book*.

Exercise 4

▶ **5.5** Ask students to look at the expressions and note the intonation. You could write the first one on the board, *On Monday?* and play it. Ask students how it is said and mark the intonation. Play the rest of the listening for students to mark intonation on the other expressions. Then ask students to repeat all of the expressions with the correct intonation.

> **Answer**
> All three expressions have a rising intonation for checking information or suggesting something.

Exercise 5

Students work in pairs. Using the *Key expressions* and, if they want, the flow chart and their own diaries, students take turns to answer the phone and make arrangements. Monitor and make sure the students are using the correct intonation to check information.

ONE-TO-ONE Start with the student playing Student A and then swap roles, so he/she gets a chance to cover all the language.

Exercise 6

▶ **5.6** Tell students they are going to listen to a call from Sergio to Elena. Ask students to look at the questions and think about the information to listen for. Students check answers with a partner. Check answers in whole-class feedback.

> **Answers**
> 1 To rearrange the meeting day and time
> 2 He can't make Tuesday.
> 3 They move it back a day (to Wednesday).

Exercise 7

Ask students to repeat the calls they made in **5**, but this time they can't make the appointment. They have to change the times. Encourage them to give a reason they can't make it. Monitor and make sure the students are using the correct intonation to check information.

Photocopiable worksheet

Download and photocopy *Unit 5 Business communication worksheet* from the teacher resources in the *Online practice*.

Talking point

Discussion

Exercise 1

Ask students what they think *upside down management* is. Ask students to read the article and the information in the organigram and discuss the question in small groups.

> **Possible answers**
> Customers are more satisfied with the service and so recommend the company. Staff are more motivated as they are allowed to show initiative, creativity and feel appreciated. Management can keep only highly-motivated, effective staff and get rid of staff who don't perform well.

Exercise 2

In the same groups, students discuss the principles. Ask them to decide if their company has any of the principles. Ask them which principles they agree or disagree with. Ask them to give reasons for their answers.

Exercise 3

Ask students to give their opinions in their groups and give reasons why upside down management would or wouldn't work in their company.

PRE-WORK LEARNERS For **2** and **3**: Students work in groups of three. Ask them to imagine a well-known company. Student A is a customer, Student B is a member of staff and Student C is a manager. Ask them to answer the questions. You could ask them to find information on the Internet about the structure of a company as preparation.

Task

Exercise 1

Students work in groups of four. Set up the situation and ask them to divide into two pairs, one making a list of arguments for, and one making a list of arguments against introducing upside down management. Give pairs time to prepare their arguments. Remind them that they will present the decisions they agree on to the class.

Exercise 2

Start the discussion, making sure the pairs present their arguments and come to an agreement on their final decision. Give the groups a time limit to present their arguments and discuss possible changes. A few minutes before the end of the task, ask the groups to reach an agreement and prepare for the presentation.

Exercise 3

Each group then presents their arguments to the class. Remind them they should give reasons for their decisions. Those listening can ask questions to clarify. You could ask them which group had the best arguments for their decisions.

ONE-TO-ONE Do the task with the student listing one set of arguments and you the other, then swap roles. Have a discussion of each of the points and come to an agreement on a decision. Ask the student to give a short presentation of the final decision at the end.

Progress test

Download and photocopy *Unit 5 Progress test* and *Speaking test* from the teacher resources in the *Online practice*.

6 Guests & visitors

Unit content

By the end of this unit, students will be able to

- talk about business travel schedules
- use articles
- find out how to address people
- welcome visitors and talk about their journey.

Context

The topic of *Guests & visitors* gives students the language to describe business travel schedules. Anybody who works, or plans to work, in business knows that no successful twenty-first century company can ignore what is happening in their industry. Valuable contacts are often made at conferences and trade fairs. To be able to go to these and exploit them for the benefit of the company, students cover the language needed for business events and to organize travel arrangements and schedules for delegates.

It is important to be able to use articles accurately. Students will cover the language to describe important conference information.

Social interaction with new contacts and customers is crucial to the success of any company. Cultural differences can lead to misunderstandings if first impressions are not good. In this unit students also learn how to address people when they meet them for the first time.

In the *Talking point*, students will have the opportunity to work out a schedule for a group of foreign visitors, proposing options for after-work activities and cultural activities and events. They will present the schedule of activities to the class.

Starting point

Do the first question with the whole class. Give them cues if they are hesitant: *What reasons could people have to visit companies? Who visits companies regularly?* Questions 2–5 can be done with the whole class or in pairs before whole-class feedback. Encourage students to develop their answers.

PRE-WORK LEARNERS Ask students to answer the following questions: *Why might someone visit a company? How might you entertain them in the evening? What are the pros and cons of travel (for business or leisure)? What can go wrong?* Students work through the list in pairs before giving feedback to the rest of the class.

Working with words

Exercise 1

Students work in pairs. Allow them a few minutes to think about and discuss the questions. Ask one or two pairs to share the ideas they came up with, in whole-class feedback.

PRE-WORK LEARNERS Students work in small groups. Give each group an area of business to concentrate on, for example, technology, transport, fashion, food, education, medicine. Ask each group to come up with four or five reasons trade fairs and conferences are important in that business area, and why people attend them.

Exercise 2

▶ **6.1** Ask students to look at the unit title and the picture and discuss who and where the people might be – what might the relationship between the people in the picture be? Tell students to read the notes and decide what information to listen for. Let students compare their answers with a partner.

Provide feedback on answers with the whole class.

> **Answer**
> 1 6.30 p.m.
> 2 Wednesday morning
> 3 airport
> 4 morning
> 5 old city
> 6 hotel
> 7 tour guide

Exercise 3

Ask students to look at the notes in **2** again and match the words in bold to definitions 1–8. Students compare answers with a partner and then check answers in whole-class feedback.

> **Answers**
> 2 facilities
> 3 auditorium
> 4 specialities
> 5 sightseeing
> 6 excursion
> 7 delegates
> 8 stands

Exercise 4

Students work in pairs, taking turns to test each other.

ONE-TO-ONE Ask the student to cover **3**. Give the definitions and he/she gives the words. You could revise next class by giving him/her the words and asking him/her to give the definitions.

Exercise 5

▶ **6.1** Refer students to the *Tip*. Ask them to match the words, which make common collocations. Play the listening again and students match the collocations to pictures A–H. If necessary, do the first one with the whole class.

Let students compare answers with a partner before doing whole-class feedback.

> **Answers**
> A meet up with (somebody)
> B check in
> C freshen up
> D pick (someone) up
> E drop (someone) off
> F show (someone) around
> G eat out
> H look around

> **DICTIONARY SKILLS**
>
> Write *travel* on the board. Ask students to work in pairs and in three minutes come up with as many words and expressions as they can to collocate with travel, for example, *travel arrangements, travel by train/plane/bus, travel alone, travel first class / business class / economy class*. Put students into small groups and ask them to find four or five collocations in their dictionary for *trip, flight* or *journey*. They check they understand each collocation and write an example sentence to show how to use it.
>
> Then put students into groups of three. Each student teaches the other students in his/her group the collocations for their group's word, and gives them examples of how to use them.
>
> **Possible answers**
> Trip: a short trip, go on a sightseeing trip, a business trip, arrange a trip, a trip abroad, a shopping trip
> Flight: a return flight, a connecting flight, a long-haul flight, a delayed flight, catch a flight, book a flight, cancel a flight
> Journey: a return journey, a five-hour journey, a ten-kilometre journey, a dangerous journey, a tiring journey, go on a journey, set out on a journey

Further practice

If students need more practice, go to *Practice file 6* on page 116 of the *Student's Book*.

Exercise 6

Ask students to work in pairs. They take turns choosing travel activities from the expressions in **5** and talk about what order they would do them in.

Ask two or three pairs to give their answers to provide whole-class feedback.

Exercise 7

Students work in pairs. Explain the situation to the students and ask if they have any experience of this. Tell students to read the information about the speakers and organize their schedules. Remind students they also have to make sure all the logistics are in place, i.e. transport, people involved, as well as places and times.

> **Possible comments on the schedules**
> The two speakers land within 15 minutes of each other so they can be picked up at the same time.
> Dr Emanuel wants time to rest and freshen up at the hotel. She can go straight to the hotel from the airport. However, Mr Sobolewski might need to go straight to the venue as his talk is at 14.00. If so, they might need to be picked up and transported in separate cars.
> Dr Emanuel will need to be collected from the hotel before her talk as she wants time to set up her equipment.
> Someone needs to confirm the number of delegates for Mr Sobolewski's talk. After his talk he will probably want to go to the hotel. In the evening he is meeting an old friend, so he will probably make his own arrangements.
> After her talk, Dr Emanuel will need to be taken out for dinner at a restaurant (with local specialities). She also leaves early on Thursday, so it would be good include a short tour of the city in the evening, either before or after dinner.
> Early in the morning a car needs to take Dr Emanuel to the airport.
> Mr Sobolewski has a free day on Thursday before his evening flight. Perhaps he could go on a tour with a guide round the city mid-morning (including a market) and have lunch somewhere nice.
> Mr Sobolewski can leave luggage at the hotel and pick it up mid-afternoon to be taken to the airport.

Photocopiable worksheet

Download and photocopy *Unit 6 Working with words worksheet* from the teacher resources in the *Online practice*.

Language at work

Exercise 1

Working in pairs, students talk about what information they expect to find on a conference website. Ask two or three pairs for their ideas for whole-class feedback.

> **Possible answers**
> Dates, times
> Venue(s)
> List of events
> Details of talks and presentations
> List of exhibitors
> How to register
> Fees
> Transportation

Exercise 2

Ask students to work in pairs, look at the website and read the information. Then tell them to think of headings for sections 2–4. Get feedback from the whole class.

> **Suggested answers**
> 2 Exhibition Centre
> 3 Getting there
> 4 On arrival

Exercise 3

Ask students to read the website in **2** again quickly. With a partner, they decide where they use or don't use articles.

Students then complete the *Language point* using the words in bold in **2**. Then do whole-class feedback.

EXTENSION Ask students to find other examples of articles and discuss why they are used. Check answers with the whole class.

Grammar reference

If students need more information, go to *Grammar reference* on page 117 of the *Student's Book*.

Exercise 4

Students work in pairs. Refer them to the *Tip*. They think of two more nouns for each category in **3**. Remind them to think of words related to work. Get feedback on answers with the whole class, eliciting why students' answers are not correct, if necessary.

EXTENSION Give students a list of words from each category and ask them to decide which take *a/an* or *the* and which take no article, for example, Russia (7), Principal's office (2) Japanese (7), students (5), juice (6), cat (1), longest (4), plane (8), man I met yesterday (3). Ask students to decide which categories in the *Language point* they would fit into.

You could ask them to give you a list of countries which take *the,* and a list of those which don't:

the: Netherlands, United States, Maldives, United Arab Emirates, Philippines (all are plurals), the Republic of China, the United Kingdom, etc.

– : France, Germany, Canada, Argentina, Egypt, etc.

Students can check their answers in an atlas or online.

Exercise 5

Ask students to read the sentences and decide which are correct. They correct the sentences that contain mistakes, with articles. Students check answers with a partner, before whole-class feedback.

PRONUNCIATION To practise pronunciation of articles, write some phrases from the sentences in **5** on the board, *giving a talk, the way to the main auditorium, there's a presentation.* Ask students what they notice about the pronunciation of the articles in the phrases – the articles usually contain a schwa because generally articles are not stressed: /ˈgɪvɪŋ ə tɔːk/ /ðə weɪ tə ðə meɪn ˌɔːrdɪˈtɔːriəm/ / ðeəz ə ˌpreznˈteɪʃn/. The exception to this is when the

following noun begins with a vowel sound, and then *the* needs to be strong form / ðiː ˈeəpɔːt/.

Ask students to read the sentences in **5** aloud, making sure they use the correct sound in the articles.

Further practice

If students need more practice, go to *Practice file 6* on page 117 of the *Student's Book*.

Exercise 6

Students work in pairs. Student A turns to page 137, and B to page 142, and they follow the instructions. You could get the Student As and Student Bs to work together in two groups, filling in the gaps in **1**. Then check the answers for each group separately before they go on to do the task.

Ask two or three pairs to ask and answer their questions in the whole-class feedback. Check they are using articles correctly, and elicit why students' answers are not correct, if necessary.

Photocopiable worksheet

Download and photocopy *Unit 6 Language at work worksheet* from the teacher resources in the *Online practice*.

Practically speaking

Exercise 1

Start by asking students how they generally address people they meet for the first time. How quickly do they use first names? How do they like to be addressed? Is it usual to use first names at work, in class?

PRE-WORK LEARNERS Ask students to imagine that someone is coming to visit their college or institution. How would they greet the visitor? What would they say and do? Have they had any experience of meeting visitors to the institution?

Exercise 2

▶ **6.2** Ask students to take turns saying the names to a partner. Play the listening for them to listen and check. You could ask them to do the exercise again.

Exercise 3

Ask students to work in small groups and discuss each of the situations. Check the answers in whole-class feedback.

PRE-WORK LEARNERS Ask students to change the first, second and fifth points to these:

- A new teacher.
- Your classmates.
- Starting a conversation with a new student to your group.

EXTENSION If all the students are from the same country, you could ask them in small groups to find out information from the Internet about what happens in the situations in **3** in other countries, as preparation for the activity. Give each group a particular country, preferably on a different continent, to get a variety of answers.

When students have got the information, they form new groups, each with one student from the original groups. They can tell each other what they have found out. Ask the class to decide which country was most different from, and which the most similar to, their own.

Exercise 4

▶ **6.3** Tell students to read the sentences. Tell them they are going to hear three conversations, then play the listening and ask them to tick the sentences they hear.

Answers
Please, call me … ✓ (1)
How would you like me to address you? ✓ (2)
Please, call me by my first name. ✓ (2)
Can I call you …? ✓ (3)

Exercise 5

Tell students they are at a conference where they don't know anyone. They must stand up and introduce themselves to different people in the class. Students can use the downloadable business cards from the teacher resources in the *Online practice* for this. You can control the activity by giving them a signal for each time you want them to move on and start a conversation with a different person. Allow students a few minutes only with each new person. Remind them to start the conversations using full names and titles, and then find out how the other person wants to be addressed.

At the end of the activity, ask three or four students what they found out about the people they met, for whole-class feedback.

ONE-TO-ONE Ask the student to introduce him/herself to you. Then introduce yourself to him/her.

Business communication

Exercise 1

Ask the students to read the information and answer the questions with a partner.

PRE-WORK LEARNERS Ask students to answer the questions about where they study.

Exercise 2

▶ **6.4** Ask students to read the agenda for Marvin's visit and decide what information to listen for. Play the listening. Students compare answers with a partner, then check answers with whole-class feedback.

Answers
Morning: Tour of the facility with Aruna Singh
Lunchtime: Lunch with Jacinta and meet Dilip Patel
Afternoon: introduction to the team

Exercise 3

▶ **6.4** Ask students to read the expressions and responses and try to match them before they listen. Play the listening again and students check the answers. If necessary, play the listening again and pause after each sentence to elicit the answer.

Answers
1 d 2 e 3 f 4 a 5 g 6 h 7 b 8 i 9 c

Exercise 4

Explain the situation to the students. Ask them to work in pairs and look at the flow chart. You could model the first exchanges with a student, if you think it is necessary. Refer the students to the *Key expressions* to help them while they are having the conversation. They can then swap roles.

Ask two or three pairs to do the conversation for whole-class feedback. Check they are using the expressions correctly, and elicit why students' answers are not correct, if necessary.

Further practice
If students need more practice, go to *Practice file 6* on page 116 of the *Student's Book*.

Exercise 5

Students work in pairs. Using the information from the *Key expressions* they have the conversation, welcoming the new person. Then they swap roles. Monitor and make sure the students are using the correct expressions.

Photocopiable worksheet
Download and photocopy *Unit 6 Business communication worksheet* from the teacher resources in the *Online practice*.

Talking point

Discussion

Exercise 1

Ask students if they have travelled to another country. Did they notice that people did things differently? Did that surprise them? How did they feel? If they haven't travelled abroad, ask them to think about the last time they stayed in a hotel. How did they feel there? What was different from being at home?

Ask them to read the information in the infographic and answer the questions.

Possible answers
Expect: Friendly hotel staff can speak their language, or a common language like English or French. Free wifi, menu with international and local dishes. TV with channels in different languages, tea & coffee making facilities, hairdryer, safety info, hotel info, telephone
Make happier: gym, swimming pool, room service

Exercise 2

▶ **6.5** Ask students to read the infographic while listening to the conversation and make a note of the ideas from it that are mentioned. Ask them to check their answers with a partner and discuss where they should expect them.

Answers
Friendly staff, free wifi, fruit bowl, ice machine, vending machine, slippers
USA, Japan, Asia

Exercise 3

Ask students to discuss the questions about cultural expectations.

Task

Exercise 1

Students work in small groups. Set up the situation and ask them to discuss and plan the schedule, using the information they are given.

Give groups time to prepare their schedules. Remind them that they will present the plan and schedule they agree on to the class.

Start the discussion, making sure the groups discuss each of the prompts and come to an agreement on their final decision. It might be a good idea to give the groups a time limit to present their arguments and discuss possible changes. A few minutes before the end of the task, ask the groups to reach agreement on the final schedule.

Each group then presents their schedule to the class. Those listening can ask questions.

EXTENSION You could ask the class which schedule they think the visitors would enjoy most and why.

ONE-TO-ONE Ask the student to prepare the schedule and present it to you.

| Progress test

Download and photocopy *Unit 6 Progress test* and *Speaking test* from the teacher resources in the *Online practice*.

Viewpoint 2

Preview

The topic of this *Viewpoint* is *Cultural communication*. In this *Viewpoint*, students begin by watching and discussing a video of four people talking about what differences they noticed when they lived and worked in a different country. Students then watch and discuss an interview with Michael Dickmann, a Senior Lecturer at Cranfield School of Management and an expert in cultural awareness in business. Finally, the students do a task which involves deciding what cultural problems are happening in three situations and why they have happened.

Exercise 1

Allow the students time to look at the list. Check they understand the meanings of *gestures*, *attitudes*, and *social behaviour* in this context. Then ask students to discuss the list with a partner. You could ask them to share anecdotes about cultural mishaps on their own travels, or when working or studying with people from other cultures.

Exercise 2

▶ 01 Tell students to think about the differences they discussed in **1**. Play the video and ask students to take notes. If necessary, pause after each speaker to allow writing time.

Answers

	Country	Differences	Changes over time
Speaker 1	Germany	colleagues very formal; quite direct but polite; meal times	changed eating habits
Speaker 2	Japan	communication; politeness; food	got used to Japanese food; etiquette didn't change
Speaker 3	UK	language differences; social differences in different parts of the country; attitudes to the natural, urban and social environment	got used to the language and accents
Speaker 4	Sweden	different attitude to working hours; meal times; levels of formality of dress	attitudes changed; became habituated

Exercise 3

Ask the students to discuss the questions with a partner. You could ask one or two pairs to report their conversation for whole-class feedback.

Exercise 4

Tell students to work in pairs and match the words and phrases 1–8 to the definitions a–h. Check answers with the whole class.

Answers
1 c **2** b **3** d **4** h **5** e **6** a **7** f **8** g

Exercise 5

▶ 02 Tell students to read A–D carefully and decide what the key words they are listening for are. Then play the whole video, telling students to number A–D in the correct order, 1–4. Let students compare answers with a partner. Then check answers with the wholeclass.

Answers
A 4 **B** 1 **C** 3 **D** 2

VIDEO SCRIPT

Part 1
Michael Dickmann is a Senior Lecturer at Cranfield School of Management.

How important is it for companies to be aware of cultural differences?
I think it's very important and the reason is you want to avoid misunderstandings between, you know, different cultures. These could be down to the way people speak and communicate, so if an English say, person says 'It's not too bad', he or she might mean 'This is excellent, this is brilliant', I as a German or others would understand 'well, it's sort of mediocre, it's not very good, is it?' OK, so you want to avoid just simply language misunderstandings, or you want to avoid cultural misunderstandings. For example, Siemens, the German multinational, had a big problem two years ago in relation to their ethics and using bribes in Africa. Now if I talk to my students here sometimes, the Nigerians call it PR, Public Relations, it's a normal thing in their business systems to pay bribes, yeah. Now it isn't a normal thing for a multinational from a western country to pay bribes. So how should people behave? So cultural understanding and ethical behaviour goes hand in hand.

Part 2
Where do you think cultural differences are most notable in a business context?
There are certain areas that are immediately noticeable in the business context, for example how polite you are and how punctual you are yeah. People realize this and they actually start to assume bits and pieces about you, if you're not punctual – you might not be disciplined or something like that – so it's important to realize those. One level deeper, in terms of norms and values, there are certain things that are really important in business life and these are much more difficult to realize. For example, there is a researcher who is called Geert Hofstede – he distinguishes between power distance, high and low. High power distance means that you wouldn't critique your boss, you would listen and even if you had a different opinion, you wouldn't voice it and you would do what your boss tells you to

do, OK? If you're from a low power distance country, like Denmark, and you go to a high power distance country, like Japan or Nigeria or South America, the countries all there have a high power distance, and you speak up against your boss, that is a big problem, OK? It's not expected and the boss feels attacked. And reverse, OK, you go from, let's say, Venezuela to Denmark or Sweden or Holland – all low power distance countries – and you don't say something when you object, and you simply do it, and then things don't turn out all right, then you can't actually say 'Well, I wasn't in favour of it, I just did it because my boss said I should do it'. No, you have to actually either voice it when the boss makes the, sort of, demand on you or it's you agreed implicitly to your boss. So both moves can create problems.

Part 3
Do you have examples of different cultural approaches in international business?

It's said there is a hamburger approach to performance management and to critiquing people. So in the US, if you made a mistake, you're being asked into the office of your boss and the boss will say something like, 'We appreciate you and it's great that you joined us and we had really good reasons and your performance is really well', so it's a sort of upper bun of a hamburger, and then he or she will continue to say, 'but last week, this is we believe you could improve, you made wrong'. So the criticism comes, which is the meat. And then, the language, the conversation will be wrapped up by approaches around, 'and we continue to trust you, we know you will be able to rectify this error and your performance will be good', so this is the lower bun, then you go out of the office.

Um, in Japan, you would only get a bun and no meat, which means you'd be asked to enter the office of your boss, the boss talks to you about how much he or she appreciates you and your performance for the company, and you'd be asked to leave again. Now the very thing that you've been asked to the boss, to meet the boss and talk to the boss, is something that makes you think, 'Oh my God, there's something wrong', so you don't get meat, but you're meant to actually realize what the meat is, yeah and it saves your face, of course.

Now in Germany, the hamburger is just the meat, so you're being asked to get into the boss's office, you're being told off and you get out again. So you have three different shapes of hamburgers yeah, and that is important to understand in terms of when you work in these countries.

Exercise 6

▶ 03 Ask students to read 1–3 and, in pairs, see what they can remember from the video. Then play Part 1 of the video for students to check their answers. Check answers with the whole class.

> **Answers**
> 1 This is excellent, this is brilliant.
> 2 It's sort of mediocre or not very good.
> 3 A bribe

Exercise 7

Ask students to discuss the questions in small groups. You could ask one or two groups to report their ideas to the whole class.

Exercise 8

▶ 04 Ask students to look at the sentences and decide what words are missing. They can compare their answers with a partner. Then play Part 2 of the video for them to check their answers. Check answers with the whole class.

> **Answers**
> 1 punctual 2 disciplined 3 high 4 low

Exercise 9

Ask students to underline the words that are true for their company and then compare answers with the rest of the class.

> **EXTRA ACTIVITY**
>
> If all the class is from the same country, ask them to discuss these questions: How would they describe the power distance in their company? Is that typical of their country? Has it changed in the last decade or two? Which countries would they describe as having a high power distance or a low one? What behaviour would they see as typical of these power distances? Which norms do they prefer and why?

PRE-WORK LEARNERS Ask students to discuss their college or university. Does it have a high or low power distance? What attitudes and behaviours demonstrate their answer? How would they describe the relationship between teachers and students?

Exercise 10

▶ 05 Ask students to read the questions and discuss the answers with a partner. Play Part 3 of the video. Check answers with the whole class.

> **Answers**
> 1 Because we can give criticism as if this was the meat in a hamburger and soften the criticism with a soft bun around it.
> 2 The manager will start positively (the upper bun), then criticise (the burger) and then finish positively again (the lower bun).
> 3 Because the manager wants you to save face.
> 4 To just give you 'the meat' and to be direct about the problem.

Exercise 11

Ask students to discuss the questions in small groups and then report back to the class. You could ask how they think 'the hamburger approach' would work in their company/ university/country.

Exercise 12

Ask students to identify the flags. Ask them to read the situations and in small groups decide exactly what the problem is and why it might have happened.

ONE-TO-ONE Ask the student if they travel abroad for work, or have contact with foreign clients, suppliers etc. Ask him/ her which countries they come from. You could ask if he/she has encountered any misunderstandings like those in the task. You could also ask him/her to find out about cultural differences between his/her own country and their clients' countries, on the Internet.

Exercise 13

Ask students to turn to page 137 and compare the explanations with theirs. Do they agree with them? Ask students how they would handle the situations to either prevent the problem from happening or to resolve the tricky situation.

Further video ideas

You can find a list of suggested ideas for how to use video in the class in the teacher resources in the *Online practice*.

Unit content

By the end of this unit, students will be able to
- talk about online security at work
- talk about rules using *must, have to, need to, can, be allowed to*
- explain him/herself clearly
- take part in a teleconference.

Context

The topic of *Working online* gives students the language to describe the security implications of working on computers. Computers are essential in every sector of twenty-first century business structure, from planning, setting up and running processes, to projects and administration, and so it is vital for all companies to be aware of online security. Cyberattacks can occur in even the most careful companies and can have a devastating effect. Companies need to be aware of best online practice to keep up-to-date and safe. To be able to discuss these areas, students cover the language needed to describe what happens when security is breached and how to create guidelines to make systems secure again.

It is important to be able to use verbs which express obligation, necessity, prohibition and permission accurately, when explaining rules and guidelines. Students are shown the differences between these verbs and are given a range to express these ideas.

Social interaction within a company is very important. The first day at work can be a daunting experience for anyone, so in this unit, students learn how to explain sequences of action clearly and helpfully. This entails giving the company rules and guidelines.

In the *Talking point*, students will have the opportunity to work in groups to write guidelines and rules concerning how employees spend time online during working hours. They will present these to the class.

Starting point

Do the first question with the whole class. Give them cues if they are hesitant: *Do you have a Smartphone? Do you usually carry a tablet, laptop, iPad? Do you use them for work, or when you're free, for example, at a concert, etc.?* Questions 2 and 3 can be done with the whole class or in pairs before whole-class feedback. Encourage students to develop their answers.

Working with words

Exercise 1

Ask students to work in pairs and discuss the questions. Ask one or two pairs to share the ideas they came up with in whole-class feedback.

Possible answer
3 Strong passwords contain a mixture of letters and numbers, upper and lower case, do not contain common words, memorable dates, names or places.

Exercise 2

Ask students to look at the title and discuss what might be in the article. Ask them to read the article and decide what the writer's purpose is. Tell them it is not necessary to understand all the words at this stage. Let students compare their answers with a partner. Provide feedback on answers with the whole class.

Answer
To convince businesses to invest in online security.

Exercise 3

Ask students to work in pairs and discuss the questions. Provide whole-class feedback for the first question and then ask two or three pairs to explain their answer to question 2 in whole-class feedback.

Answers
1 The writer supports the view by describing the Spamhaus's cyberattack, the fact that 79% of executives are not confident about their company's level of online protection, and the lack of spending by companies on cybersecurity.

PRE-WORK LEARNERS You could ask students about their own online security, and how confident they feel about it. How do they stay secure?

Exercise 4

Students work in pairs. If necessary, check the first answer with the whole class. Then tell students to find the words in the article in **2** to work out the meanings. Check the answers in whole-class feedback.

EXTENSION Ask students to take turns to practise the vocabulary. Student A gives the definitions and Student B gives the words. They then swap roles.

ONE-TO-ONE Ask the student to cover **4.** Give the definitions and he/she gives the words. You could revise next class by giving the student the words and asking him/her to give the definitions.

Exercise 5

Ask students to discuss the questions with a partner. You could ask two or three pairs to tell the class about what happened to them or anyone they know, if they are willing to.

Exercise 6

▶ **7.1** Tell students they are going to listen to three people talking about online security. Tell them to read the types of online security, which they are going to match with each person. Play the listening. Let them compare answers with a partner. Check answers in whole-class feedback.

Exercise 7

▶ **7.1** Ask students to look at the verbs 1–7 and the nouns a–g. Play the listening again. Students work in pairs to match the collocations.

PRONUNCIATION To practise word stress in collocations, write the collocation *upgrade software* on the board. Ask students which syllables are stressed and mark them on the board. Ask students to mark the stressed syllables in the rest of the collocations. Students take turns to practise saying them.

Exercise 8

Students work in pairs, taking turns to ask and answer questions, using the collocations in **7**. Ask them to extend their answers by giving reasons. Ask two or three pairs to ask and answer their questions for whole-class feedback.

PRE-WORK LEARNERS Ask students to make and answer questions using the collocations from **7** about their own personal online security.

DICTIONARY SKILLS

Put students into three groups, A, B, C. Ask group A to find three or four words that go with *cyber-*, group B to find three or four words that go with *online*, and group C to find three or four words that go with *computer*. They should find the definitions and make a sentence to show the word in context. Then regroup into new groups of A, B, C and each student teaches the others in their group their words.

Possible answers

Cyber – attack, bully, café, crime, naut
Online – security, dating, banking, post something online, go online, be online
Computer – game, hacker, literacy, science, error, software, virus, glitch

Further practice

If students need more practice, go to *Practice file 7* on page 118 of the *Student's Book*.

Exercise 9

Students work in pairs. They could think of several important areas where companies have guidelines for working online, for example, password security, personal use, sending information out to clients/freelancers, downloading programmes or surfing the Internet.

Remind students to use the words and expressions from **4** and **7**. Monitor, checking that students are using the words correctly.

PRE-WORK LEARNERS Ask students to imagine they work in a well-known company and write the guidelines, coming up with a minimum of five. They could find information about the company on the Internet.

ONE-TO-ONE Ask the student to write the guidelines. He/she then presents them to you, giving reasons for his/her choices.

EXTENSION Ask the pairs to split up and make small groups of four to six. Then each student presents their guidelines to the group, giving reasons for their choices. You could ask each group to come up with a group list of five or six guidelines to present to the whole class.

Photocopiable worksheet

Download and photocopy *Unit 7 Working with words worksheet* from the teacher resources in the *Online practice*.

Language at work

Exercise 1

With a partner, students discuss the prompts. They could think of an example of a rule for each one. Ask two or three pairs for their ideas for whole-class feedback.

PRE-WORK LEARNERS Ask students to discuss the rules in their school or college. Which rules do they find surprising, if any?

Exercise 2

Ask students to read the rules and answer the questions. How are the rules at their company different from the company rules here?

PRE-WORK LEARNERS Ask students to think about the rules in their school or college. Has there ever been a breach of security? What happened? Are there any ways they think security could be improved?

Exercise 3

Ask students to read the rules in **2** again quickly. With a partner, they then complete the *Language point* using the words in bold. Then do whole-class feedback.

Answers
2	have to	5	mustn't
3	need to	6	are allowed to
4	are not allowed to	7	can

Grammar reference

If students need more information, go to *Grammar reference* on page 119 of the *Student's Book*.

Exercise 4

Students work individually. Refer them to the *Tip*. They underline the correct verb in italics. Let them check their answers with a partner. Check answers in whole-class feedback.

Answers
1 are allowed to
2 have to
3 mustn't
4 can

Exercise 5

Students work in pairs. Ask them to read the sentences and complete them so they are true for them. They then take turns giving their sentences. Ask them to find out more information about the rules and policies by asking questions using the verbs in the *Language point*, and whether their partner thinks they are successful or not and why. Monitor, checking they are using the verbs correctly.

Check by asking some pairs to report back on what they thought were the most sensible, interesting or surprising rules and policies, for whole-class feedback.

PRE-WORK LEARNERS Ask students to talk about their school or college, and decide what rules and policies they expect the college to have.

ALTERNATIVE If students all work for the same company, ask them to think about different areas of business, for example, computer software, car manufacturing, transport

companies. Students work in pairs, choose a company in the area and imagine they have an online security consultancy firm. They have been asked to provide security measures for the company they have chosen. Students make a list of the measures and the reasons for suggesting them. Then they present their ideas to the class.

Further practice

If students need more practice, go to *Practice file 7* on page 119 of the *Student's Book*.

Exercise 6

▶ 7.2 Explain the situation to the students. A new employee is shown to her desk. She has some questions about rules in the company. Play the listening. Students discuss, in pairs, which rules the speakers discussed. Check answers in whole-class feedback.

Answers
The rules they discuss are related to creating a password and making personal calls.

Exercise 7

▶ 7.2 Students listen again and write down the three questions they hear. Let them compare their answers with a partner, and then check the answers in whole-class feedback.

Answers
1 Do I have to use a password with the laptop?
2 Am I allowed to choose my own?
3 Can I make personal calls from this phone?

PRONUNCIATION Ask students to listen to the questions again and listen for the rising/falling intonation. Ask them to repeat. You could write the first question on the board and ask them to tell you what they hear, and then mark the stress and intonation to show them how.

Answers
1 Do I have to use a password with the laptop?
2 Am I allowed to choose my own?
3 Can I make personal calls from this phone?

Exercise 8

Explain the situation to the students. They work in pairs and follow the instructions. Give students some time to prepare the rules and questions.

Provide whole-class feedback by asking two or three pairs to have the conversation in front of the class.

ALTERNATIVE You could put all the Student As and Bs together in two groups. The As come up with the rules for the company, and the Bs come up with the questions. Then divide them into AB pairs and they follow the instructions for the role-play.

PRE-WORK LEARNERS Students imagine they work in a (real) company. They could find out information about the company from the Internet, as different companies may have different levels of security.
Set up the role-play as suggested above.

Photocopiable worksheet

Download and photocopy *Unit 7 Language at work worksheet* from the teacher resources in the *Online practice*.

Practically speaking

Exercise 1

Start by asking students how often they register with websites. Do they register for work or for personal things? Ask them what sorts of websites they register with, then ask them to discuss with a partner the questions about the information they do or don't give to websites.

Ask two or three pairs for their responses for whole-class feedback.

Exercise 2

▶ **7.3** Explain the situation to the students. Ask them to think about when they have registered with a website and put the stages in order before you play the listening. They then listen and check their answers.

Answers
2 Click 'register' button
3 Receive temporary password
4 Change temporary password
5 Agree to terms and conditions
6 Start using the site

Exercise 3

▶ **7.3** Ask students to read the sentences and write in the missing words. Then play the listening again for them to check the answers.

Answers
1 begin	4 Once
2 then	5 now
3 Next	6 before

PRONUNCIATION Remind students that when they give instructions, they should pause after each instruction to give the listener time to carry it out. Ask them to take turns reading the sentences to a partner, explaining how to register. For example, *OK. // So start by filling in these details first. // And then click register. // Then it'll email you a temporary password // which you can change. // Once you've done that // you can log on …*, etc.

Exercise 4

Students work in pairs. Tell them to choose one of the processes and spend a few minutes getting the sequence in order so they can tell their partner about it. Refer students to the *Tip*. When they are explaining the process, they can give reasons for the way something is done, and their partner should ask questions to find out more information.

Monitor, checking they are giving clear explanations and pausing so their partner can follow them easily.

EXTENSION Ask students to find another partner and either tell the new partner about their process or explain their first partner's process.

PRE-WORK LEARNERS Ask students to think of a website they have logged on to previously, for example, Facebook, and explain to a partner what to do to log on.

Business communication

Exercise 1

Ask students to look at the picture and discuss the questions with a partner. Discuss the answers in whole-class feedback.

Possible answers
Pros: You can talk to people who are not near, for example in another city or country.
There are economies of time – people don't have to travel to a meeting and so miss work.
Cons: Sometimes there are misunderstandings when you aren't face-to-face.
It's hard to build up a good working relationship if you don't meet the other people.

PRE-WORK LEARNERS Ask students to imagine what taking part in a teleconference is like, how easy it would be to explain something complex, or take notes, for example, and what advantages and disadvantages it could have.

Exercise 2

▶ **7.4** Explain the situation to students. Tell them to read the questions to see what information to listen for. Explain there are three parts to the teleconference. Play the listening. Students answer the questions individually and then compare their answers with a partner.

Answers
1 Lauren
2 Too quiet
3 Raymond and Helmi
4 Vance asks Raymond to speak first and then Helmi.
5 If they have any questions
6 An email with all the main points from their meeting

Exercise 3

▶ **7.4** Ask students to read the expressions for starting, managing and ending the call and try to put them in order before they listen.

Play the listening again and students check the answers with a partner. If necessary, listen again and pause after each sentence to elicit the answer in whole-class feedback.

Answers
Starting
2 We're just waiting for Raymond.
1 Lauren is here with me.
3 Your line isn't very good. Can you speak up?
Managing
5 Lauren, can you speak first?
7 Would you like to comment?
4 OK, let's begin. Today, I want to discuss …
6 Raymond, can you speak first? And then Helmi, you can speak next.
Ending
8 I think that covers everything.
11 Thank you everyone for coming.
9 Are there any questions before we finish?
10 I'll sum up the main points in an email.

Further practice

If students need more practice, go to *Practice file 7* on page 118 of the *Student's Book*.

Exercise 4

Explain the situation to the students. They work individually. After reading the email, they make some notes for the meeting.

Exercise 5

Students work in small groups. Using their notes from **4** and the *Key expressions*, they have the conversation. If students have mobile phones or Skype, they could call each other. It might be a good idea to have them sit back to back to imitate a phone call.

Monitor, making sure the students are using the correct expressions.

Ask two or three groups to do the conversation for whole-class feedback. Check they are using the expressions correctly.

ONE-TO-ONE Ask the student to prepare for the call as instructed in **4.** Then have the call. Make sure he/she leads and manages the call.

Photocopiable worksheet

Download and photocopy *Unit 7 Business communication worksheet* from the teacher resources in the *Online practice*.

Talking point

Discussion

Exercise 1

As a lead-in, ask students if they work with a computer at work, and how much time they spend online. Ask them to read the information in the infographic and say which is the most and least surprising piece of data, and why.

Exercise 2

Ask students to work in small groups and discuss the questions. Ask two or three groups to report back for whole-class feedback.

Exercise 3

Ask students to work in pairs and discuss the questions. Ask a few pairs to report back for whole-class feedback.

PRE-WORK LEARNERS Students can discuss how much time they spend online doing other things when they are supposed to be studying.

Task

Exercise 1

Students work in groups of four. Set up the situation and ask them to think of four or five areas that need to be discussed.

Give groups time to prepare their suggestions.

> **Possible areas**
> Length of time for personal use
> Sites allowed or not allowed to visit
> Things not allowed to do (buying things, sending personal emails, etc.)
> Watching movies, playing games, etc.

Exercise 2

Divide the groups into two pairs, A and B. Start the task, making sure the pairs discuss each of the areas they suggested in **1** and come to an agreement on their guidelines and rules. It might be a good idea to give the groups a time limit to work on this part of the task. A few minutes before the end of the task, ask the groups to reach agreement on the guidelines and rules.

Exercise 3

The pairs join up again. Each pair then presents their guidelines and rules to the group. Those listening can ask questions to get more details. The whole group then works together to find areas where they have similar views and discuss differences. As a group they try to reach agreement on a final set of guidelines and rules to present to the whole class.

Then each group presents their guidelines. You could ask the class which set of guidelines and rules they think would be most successful, and why.

EXTENSION You could ask the students to create their own survey about online use at work / in college in small groups. Then they interview the students in the other groups.

When they have all the information, they could create and present their own infographic. They could also present three or four guidelines which arise from the information in the infographic.

ONE-TO-ONE Ask the student to prepare the guidelines and present them to you.

Progress test

Download and photocopy *Unit 7 Progress test* and *Speaking test* from the teacher resources in the *Online practice*.

8 Finance

Context

The topic of *Finance* gives students the language to describe the financial aspects of a project. All companies need to be aware of how to source the capital needed to start a business or finance a project. It is not only essential to raise money for a business, but also to consider the investors and their expectations. To do this, students cover the language needed to discuss budgets, financial forecasts, dividends, commission and equity.

It is important to be able to use future forms accurately when predicting results and possibilities. Students will describe a wide range of predictions about companies, and wider national and global events which can affect companies and their finances. They go on to discuss setting up an office in another country.

In this unit, students will learn about different functions for the verb form *will*. This will cover predictions, promises, making decisions and giving conditions. They will go on to practise presenting visual information about the future, using all of the future forms covered in the unit.

In the *Talking point*, the students will discuss investment opportunities and crowdfunding. Each student presents a crowdfunding opportunity and they all decide which idea is the most attractive investment opportunity. They then discover which of the four possibilities was the most successful.

Starting point

Do the first question with the whole class. Give them cues if they are hesitant: *What is the job title of the person – accountant, finance director, line manager,* etc.? The second and third questions can be done in pairs before whole-class feedback. Encourage students to develop their answers.

PRE-WORK LEARNERS Ask students to think about a real company. Who do they think deals with finances? You could ask them to find out what the names of the people who deal with money in a company are, for example, the Accounts Department, the Finance Director, the directors, an accountant, a line manager, etc.

Working with words

Exercise 1

Allow students a few minutes to think about the different ways of raising money and then ask them to discuss their ideas in groups and come up with some pros and cons for each.

Possible answers

	Pros	Cons
From a bank	A secure loan	The bank needs all your financial history and will charge interest
From a rich relative or friend	No interest to pay	May cause problems with family or friend if you can't pay back
From a business investor	Could benefit from the investor's experience	Will want a share of the company
Find a business partner	You can share the pressure	You only get half the profits and you may disagree
Use lots of credit cards	Fast way to get the finance	High interest rates
Save up the money	No interest and you are independent	You have to wait before you can start and someone might start a similar business in the meantime

Exercise 2

Ask students to read the questions and then the article. Tell students it's not necessary to understand all the words, only the general sense. Provide whole-class feedback.

Answers
1 Lauren Peers and Mike Thompson raised the money for their businesses through crowdfunding sites.
2 Lauren gave one investor ownership of a cat, and Mike had to give away a 40% share in the business.

Exercise 3

Ask students to compare ideas in their groups. For example, *Why is crowdfunding sometimes a good idea? What sort of businesses would find it useful? What problems could there be?* After the group work, provide feedback with the whole class by asking someone from each group for their group's ideas.

Exercise 4

Ask students to read the article in **2** again quickly and notice the words in bold. If necessary, do the first answer with the whole class and then ask them to complete the other sentences individually. Let them compare answers with a partner before doing whole-class feedback.

Answers

1	loan	6	financial forecasts
2	capital	7	commission
3	budding entrepreneurs	8	shares
4	potential investors	9	equity
5	dividends		

Exercise 5

Students work in pairs by covering the answers in **4** and taking turns to read out the definitions and remember the words.

PRONUNCIATION Ask students to mark the stress on the answers in **4**. Monitor, checking students are stressing the right syllables.

Answers

capital
budding entrepreneurs
potential investors
dividends

financial forecasts
commission
equity

ONE-TO-ONE You read the definition and the student gives the word or words. You could revise in the next class by reading the word(s) and asking him/her for the definition.

Exercise 6

Ask students to read the article in **2** again quickly and complete the sentences with the missing preposition. Check answers in whole-class feedback. Then ask students to ask and answer the questions with a partner. Monitor, checking they are using the correct prepositions.

Answers
1 for
2 back
3 towards
4 out

PRE-WORK LEARNERS Ask students to imagine they work for different well-known companies and answer the questions. You could ask them to look up the information for each on the Internet as preparation for the exercise.

Exercise 7

Students work in pairs. Tell them to scan the article in **2** and find what the numbers refer to. Remind students what scanning is, i.e. reading a text quickly to find specific pieces of information like a number, time, name, etc. Check the answers in whole-class feedback.

Answers

100,000 – the capital Lauren Peers needed to open her business
60 – the number of days in which Lauren raised £110,000
7,000 – the number of bookings at the cat café on the first day
£20,000 – the amount one woman paid Lauren in return for a cat
98 – the number of Mike's investors
£80,000 – the amount the investors paid Mike
40% – the share in the company that Mike gave away for investment
5% – the approximate commission some crowdfunding sites take for their services

DICTIONARY SKILLS
Ask students to check their dictionaries to find the prepositions that can go with the following verbs and expressions: *spend money, save, waste money, borrow money, take money, owe, get money*. Then they can write a sentence for each expression. You could ask them to say their sentence, without the expression, and ask a partner which expression is missing.

Possible answers

spend money on	take money out (of)
save up for	owe money to/for
waste money on	get money off
borrow money for/from	

Further practice

If students need more practice, go to *Practice file 8* on page 120 of the *Student's Book*.

Exercise 8

Students work in small groups and follow the instructions. Give students time to choose the business idea and come up with the answers to the questions. You could give them a time limit. Remind them that they will give a presentation of their business idea and plans to raise money. Remind them of the time limit a few minutes before you want them to end.

ONE-TO-ONE Ask the student to think of a new idea that would benefit his/her business. Tell him/her that he/she has to raise the money via a crowdfunding website. Ask the student to prepare a presentation to give to the board of his/her company about the new idea, the investors he/she would like to attract and what the investors can hope to receive in return for their investment.

Exercise 9

Each group presents their ideas to the class. Those listening should try to come up with some questions to get more information. The class decides which group is offering the best investment opportunity.

Further practice

Download and photocopy *Unit 8 Working with words worksheet* from the teacher resources in the *Online practice*.

Language at work

Exercise 1

Ask students to make a list in groups. Ask one or two groups to give feedback to the whole class.

> **Possible answers**
> heating, training, stationery, coffee, office cleaning, decorating, travel to meetings, meetings with customers, etc.

PRE-WORK LEARNERS Tell students to imagine they work for a (real) company. Put the students into small groups. Tell each group to choose a department and think about the expenses it would have and make the list. They can then tell the other groups their list. Which expenses do all departments have, and which ones are for particular departments?

Exercise 2

Tell students to look at the table and answer the questions. Let them compare answers with a partner. Check the answers in whole-class feedback.

> **Answers**
> The department is over budget on overtime and travel. It can still spend money on wages, training, recruitment and legal fees.

Exercise 3

▶ 8.1 Explain that students are going to listen to three parts of a budget meeting. Tell them to write down which budget expenses are being discussed. Students compare answers with a partner and then do whole-class feedback.

> **Answers**
> Part 1: wages and overtime
> Part 2: travel and training
> Part 3: travel, recruitment and wages

Exercise 4

▶ 8.1 Ask students to read the sentence beginnings 1–7 and match them to a–g to complete the sentences. Let students compare answers with a partner. Play the listening again for them to check the answers.

> **Answers**
> 2 c 3 g 4 a 5 e 6 f 7 d

Exercise 5

Refer students to the *Tip*. Ask them to read the answers in **4** and use sentence numbers 1–7 to complete a–c in the *Language point*. Let students check answers with a partner, before whole-class feedback.

> **Answers**
> a Sentence 1 b (*be going to*)
> b Very certain in sentence 6 f (*will definitely*)
>   Fairly certain in sentence 4 a (*will probably*)
>   Less certain in sentence 7 d (*'ll possibly*)
> c 2 c (*might*), 3 g (*may*) and 5 e (*could*)
> The main verbs in all the sentences are in the infinitive without *to* form.

Grammar reference

If students need more information, go to *Grammar reference* on page 121 of the *Student's Book*.

Exercise 6

Tell students to underline the correct form of the verbs. If necessary, do the first sentence with the whole class. Remind them that in one sentence both forms are possible. Students work in pairs. Check with whole-class feedback, eliciting why students' answers are incorrect, if necessary.

> **Answers**
> 1 're going to
> 2 may
> 3 'll definitely
> 4 might not
> 5 's going to
> 6 could/might
> 7 definitely won't
> 8 could

Further practice

If students need more practice, go to *Practice file 8* on page 121 of the *Student's Book*.

Exercise 7

Students work individually to think about their own predictions for the prompts. Then put students in small groups to discuss the predictions. Monitor, checking students are using the correct future form. Ask two or three groups for predictions in whole-class feedback.

PRE-WORK LEARNERS For the first prompt, ask students to talk about their own budget/spending over the coming year. If students don't know about tax rates, retirement age, pensions and interest rates, you could ask them to find the information on the Internet.

Exercise 8

Explain the situation and tell students to work in groups of four. The groups divide into two pairs and follow the instructions. Pair A turns to page 137 and pair B turns to page 142. While pair A is giving the presentation of their budget breakdown, pair B must listen and come up with questions about the details of the budget. The pairs should try to reach an agreement on how the budget should be split between each expense, and whether each expense is realistic or not. Provide whole-class feedback by getting one or two groups to report back on their meeting.

ONE-TO-ONE Ask the student to look at the information on page 137 and prepare their presentation. You look at the information on page 142 and prepare questions to ask after he/she has given his/her presentation.

Photocopiable worksheet

Download and photocopy *Unit 8 Language at work worksheet* from the teacher resources in the *Online practice*.

Practically speaking

Exercise 1

Start by asking students to read the sentences and, with a partner, decide what each situation might be. Do not correct answers here, as they come in the listening in **2**. Accept all possible answers at this stage.

Exercise 2

▶ **8.2** Explain that students are going to listen to four conversations and check if their ideas in **1** were correct. Play the listening and let students compare answers in pairs before checking answers with the whole class.

Exercise 3

Ask students to match the sentences from **1** to the uses of *will*. Check answers in whole-class feedback.

PRONUNCIATION Play listening **8.2** again and ask students to notice how *will* is pronounced. Ask them to mark the sentence stress. Students take turns practising saying the sentences.

Exercise 4

Ask students to work in pairs to make four short conversations with the prompt sentences. Ask them to practise saying the sentences. Tell students to work in new pairs and practise their own and their partner's conversations. Provide feedback by asking two or three pairs to perform their conversations for the class.

Business communication

Exercise 1

Ask students to read the information in the slides and answer the questions. At this stage, accept all possible answers, as the answers come in the listening in **2**.

Exercise 2

▶ **8.3** Ask students to listen to the presentation and check their answers to **1**. Play the listening. Ask students to number the slides in the correct order. Let students compare answers with a partner and then check with the whole class.

Exercise 3

▶ **8.3** Ask students to look at the expressions before they listen and try to match them to the slides. Play the listening again, students check their answers. If necessary, listen again and pause after each sentence to elicit the answer.

Exercise 4

Students work in pairs. Tell them this is a practice for their own presentation in **5**. Ask them to look at the slides A–D in **1**, the answers in **3** and refer them to the *Key expressions*. They then take turns presenting the slides. Monitor, making sure the students are clear when presenting the information on the slides and that they are using the language from the *Key expressions*.

Exercise 5

Students discuss the questions. Check their ideas in whole-class feedback. Ask them to come up with two or three reasons for their choice.

> **Possible answer**
> Investing in student accommodation is a good idea as the number of students, and therefore the demand for accommodation, is going to increase.

Further practice

If students need more practice, go to *Practice file 8* on page 120 of the *Student's Book*.

Exercise 6

Students work in pairs. Tell them to prepare a short presentation with the information on the relevant pages. Student A turns to page 138, and B to page 143. Give them a time limit for the preparation. They then decide whether it is a good investment or not and give their reasons. Provide whole-class feedback by getting two or three pairs to give presentations.

ONE-TO-ONE Ask the student to give a presentation using all the information on both slides on pages 138 and 143.

Photocopiable worksheet

Download and photocopy *Unit 8 Business communication worksheet* from the teacher resources in the *Online practice*.

Talking point

Discussion

Exercise 1

Ask students to look at the pictures and work out what they show. Ask students to read the article and discuss the pros and cons of each idea with a partner.

Possible answers

	Pros	Cons
Fish on wheels	An unusual toy for people who have everything; not a lot of money required.	Has no real use.
MiRing	You never miss a call.	The light and the vibration could be annoying. A lot of money needed in a very short time.
New York City Opera	Cultural and historical company, people get something for the money they invest.	Opera is not very popular with a lot of people, it's expensive to produce so it needs a huge amount of money.
Form1	Affordable, professional 3D printer for home use.	A lot of money needed. How useful is a 3D printer?

Exercise 2

Students can discuss the question in small groups before whole-class feedback.

Exercise 3

This exercise could be run as a whole-class discussion.

Task

Exercise 1

Students work in groups of four. Ask each student in the group to choose one of the crowdfunding ideas from the article.

Exercise 2

Give students time to each prepare a two-minute presentation following the instructions, making sure they cover all the points. You could suggest they prepare in AA and BB pairs if you think it is necessary for weaker students.

Exercise 3

Each student then gives their presentation to the group. Remind those listening that they can ask questions at the end of each presentation, not during.

After all four presentations, the group decides on the most attractive investment. Then ask each group to report to the class on the investment they chose and their reasons for choosing it.

Exercise 4

Finally, turn to page 138 and find out what happened to each crowdfunding idea. Which students chose the most successful idea?

ONE-TO-ONE Ask the student to choose one of the crowdfunding ideas and give his/her presentation. When they have given the presentation, turn to page 138 and find out what happened to each. Did they choose the most successful idea?

Progress test

Download and photocopy *Unit 8 Progress test* and *Speaking test* from the teacher resources in the *Online practice*.

9 Logistics

Context

The topic of *Logistics* gives students the language to discuss the practical organization that is needed to make a complicated plan successful when many different people and equipment are involved. All companies need to have systems in place to efficiently organize and plan how its resources can make it successful. Examples of resources include human resources (the staff), technical systems and services, transport and administration. Learners cover the language needed to discuss logistics and supply chains, covering importing, transporting, storing and keeping track of goods.

It is important to be able to have conversations with customers and suppliers. To do this, students will learn how to use direct and indirect questions appropriately to achieve successful outcomes in conversations. Students will also tackle the difference between *say* and *tell*.

In this unit, students will also learn how to place and handle orders, including where they have not arrived on the designated date. They will have the opportunity to role-play situations, both as a customer and supplier, and resolve a problem concerning an order.

In the *Talking point*, students will discuss the increasing phenomenon of shadow work. They will have the opportunity to discuss what it is and the effect it has on work–life balance. They will present a list of jobs that could become shadow work and the benefits this could have for customers.

Starting point

Do the first question with the whole class. Give them cues if they are hesitant: *Have you heard the word? Where have you seen the word?* The second question can be done with the whole class or in pairs before whole-class feedback. Encourage students to develop their answers.

Answer

Logistics is the practical organization that is needed to make a complicated plan successful when a lot of people and equipment are involved.
It can also be defined as the business of transporting and delivering goods.
From http://www.oxfordlearnersdictionaries.com/

Working with words

Exercise 1

Allow students a few minutes to think about the questions and then ask them to discuss their ideas in small groups to come up with a list.

Possible answer

The list could include cost, time, size of order, packing materials, how fragile the goods are, customs and laws on certain goods.

Exercise 2

Ask students to look at the picture in the article. Ask them what type of business they think Emad Razavi runs. What do they think some of the challenges are? Tell them to read the questions and then the article. Tell students it's not necessary to understand all the words, only the general sense. Provide feedback on answers with the whole class.

Answers

1 Sourcing the goods. Transportation. Storage and showroom.
2 Sourcing the goods: buying them from nomadic tribes and through middlemen. He has to trust them.
Transportation: How to transport them depending on the country they are coming from.
Storage and showroom: Each rug is unique so he needs records on each one.

Exercise 3

Ask students to read the article in **2** again quickly and match the definitions to the words in bold. Let students compare answers with a partner. Check answers in whole-class feedback.

Answers

1	supply chain	6	middlemen
2	handmade	7	shipment
3	inventory	8	run low on
4	origin	9	keep track of
5	showroom		

EXTENSION Dictate these words from the article and ask students to mark the stress. Then they practise by taking turns saying the words: *business, imports (v) supply chain,* _handmade, inventory, origin, showroom, middlemen, shipment, contacts, transports (v), condition, warehouse, client._

ONE-TO-ONE To revise these words, give the student a word and ask him/her to give the definition.

Exercise 4

Ask students to discuss the points in small groups. Provide whole-class feedback by asking different groups to report back on each point.

PRE-WORK LEARNERS Students work in small groups. Ask them to imagine they are in different businesses supplying different goods, for example, foodstuffs, electrical goods, clothes, technological items. Give them some time to prepare ideas on how each point is important to their business. If necessary, they could find some information on the Internet.
Ask them to discuss each point in their group and then provide feedback by asking them to report back on how one of the points affects their business.

Exercise 5

▶ **9.1** Tell students they are going to listen to another business owner talking about his business. Elicit the areas that the article in **2** covered, and ask students to read the questions. Play the listening. Let students compare answers with a partner. Check answers in whole-class feedback.

Answers
1 They both run businesses which specialize and provide a personal touch.
2 with bar codes
3 He sometimes uses a tracking facility.

Exercise 6

▶ **9.1** Ask students to read the sentences and complete them with the missing words. Play the listening again for them to check their answers. Check answers in whole-class feedback.

Answers
1 in
2 out
3 on
4 low
5 up

Exercise 7

Students work in pairs. Tell them to look at the answers in **6** and match them to the meanings. Check the answers in whole-class feedback.

Answers
to have a product available for sale: to keep in stock
to not have many: to run low (on something)
to not have any: to run out (of something)
to buy a lot of something: to stock up on
to be waiting for a delivery: to be on order

Further practice

If students need more practice, go to _Practice file 9_ on page 122 of the _Student's Book_.

Exercise 8

Students work in pairs and follow the instructions. Give them time to choose the product and work out the supply chain. If they have problems coming up with a product or company, you could suggest a company like Amazon, or one known in the area, or something like a laptop computer. You could give them a time limit. Students then take turns describing their product supply chain to their partner.

Provide whole-class feedback by asking two or three students to report to the class.

EXTENSION You could ask students to change partners and either explain their product supply chain again or their first partner's supply chain. They could do this two or three more times for extra practice.

Photocopiable worksheet

Download and photocopy _Unit 9 Working with words worksheet_ from the teacher resources in the _Online practice_.

Language at work

Exercise 1

Ask students to work in pairs and discuss the question. Ask one or two pairs to feed back to the whole class.

Possible answers
A air freight: advantage – speed; disadvantage – cost
B cargo ship: advantage – ability to transport larger containers, etc.; disadvantage – slow
C truck/articulated lorry: advantage – delivery to door; disadvantage – traffic delays

Exercise 2

▶ **9.2** Tell students to listen to the customer enquiry and answer the questions. Play the listening. Let students compare answers with a partner. Check the answers in whole-class feedback.

Answers
1 They want to deliver documents.
2 They are going to use air transportation

Exercise 3

▶ **9.2** Tell students to read the pairs of questions. Play the listening. Students tick the five questions they hear. Get them to compare answers with a partner and then do whole-class feedback.

Answers
1 a 2 a 3 a 4 b 5 b

Exercise 4

Ask students to read the questions in **3** and decide which are direct and which are indirect. Let students compare answers with a partner and then check answers with the whole class.

Answers
The **b** questions are direct. The **a** questions are indirect.
1 a I was wondering if I could get a quote.
2 a I'd like to know how much it costs to send a package.
3 a Could you tell me how big the package is?
4 a Do you have any idea how long that takes?
5 a Would you mind telling me what the price is?

Exercise 5

Ask students to read the questions in **3** again and choose the correct options to complete the *Language point*. They then check answers with a partner before whole-class feedback.

Answers
1 more
2 indirect
3 if
4 before

PRONUNCIATION Write the first indirect question on the board, *I was wondering if I could get a quote*. Ask students to listen to how the phrase *I was wondering if* is chunked, /aɪwəzwʌndrɪŋif/ as one word. Ask students to practise saying the other indirect question chunks as if they're one word:
I'd like to know … /aɪdlaɪktənəʊ/
Could you tell me … /kədjutelmi/
Do you have any idea … /dəjuəveniaɪˈdɪə/
Would you mind telling me … /wədjumaɪndtelɪŋmi/

Grammar reference
If students need more information, go to *Grammar reference* on page 123 of the *Student's Book*.

Exercise 6

Students work in pairs. Tell them to think of one direct and one indirect question for each of the situations. Remind students about chunking the indirect questions. Check answers in whole-class feedback.

Possible answers
1 What time would you like the delivery? / Could you tell me when you would like the delivery?
2 Why haven't they arrived yet? / I'd like to know why they haven't arrived yet.
3 Can you speak up? / Would you mind speaking up?
4 Who did you speak to? / Do you have any idea who you spoke to?

EXTENSION Ask students to make short, two- to three-line, conversations using direct and indirect questions. Students can practise by taking turns to ask and answer the questions.

Further practice
If students need more practice, go to *Practice file 9* on page 123 of the *Student's Book*.

Exercise 7

Students work in pairs. They turn to the relevant page and follow the instructions. Student A turns to page 139, and B stays on page 61. They work individually to think about their own information for the phone calls, making questions to get the information they need.

Then students have the phone calls. If there's room, ask the students to sit back to back for the calls. Monitor, checking students are using both question forms.

Photocopiable worksheet
Download and photocopy *Unit 9 Language at work worksheet* from the teacher resources in the *Online practice*.

Practically speaking

Exercise 1

▶ **9.3** Start by explaining the situation and asking students to listen and answer the questions. Play the listening. Check answers in whole-class feedback.

Answers
The employee reports on a meeting with a client. The manager decides to meet the client next week on Friday.

Exercise 2

▶ **9.3** Ask students to complete the sentences with *say* or *tell*. Let them compare answers with a partner, then play the listening again to check answers with the whole class.

Answers
1 tell
2 says
3 tell
4 say
5 say
6 tell

Exercise 3

Ask students to match the meaning of *say* and *tell* in the sentences from **2** to the definitions a–f. Check answers in whole-class feedback.

Answers
b 4   c 2   d 5   e 6   f 3

Exercise 4

Ask students to work in pairs. Refer them to the *Tip*. Ask students to have the conversation, following the instructions and using the flow chart. Monitor, checking they are using the question forms and *say* and *tell* correctly.

Tell students to swap partners and go through the flow chart conversation again.

Provide whole-class feedback by asking two or three pairs to perform their conversations for the class.

DICTIONARY SKILLS
Dictate these parts of expressions; *… a joke, … something funny, … a story, … what you mean, … (something) out loud, … a lie, … somebody to do something, that was a very unkind thing to …* Ask students to decide which expressions go with *say* and which with *tell*.

Tell them to check their answers in their dictionaries.

Answers
Tell: *… a joke, … a story, … a lie, … somebody to do something*
Say: *… something funny, … what you mean, … (something) out loud, that was very unkind thing to …*

EXTRA ACTIVITY
Ask students to prepare a message that they would leave on someone's voicemail. They then read it to their partner, who takes notes. Afterwards, the listener has to report the message back. This means that the listener has to use *say* and *tell* and also ensures that he/she took the correct information. You may need to remind students about the tense and time word changes for reporting speech.

Business communication

Exercise 1

Tell students to look at the title and the picture and guess what the people could be doing. Check students understand what a *motherboard* is – it's the main board of a computer, containing all the circuits. Then ask students to read the email and answer the questions. Let them check their answers with a partner. Check answers in whole-class feedback.

> **Answers**
> 1 2,000 motherboards
> 2 yes
> 3 asap (as soon as possible)
> 4 on account

Exercise 2

Ask students to read the email in **1** again and underline the phrases for placing an order. Check answers with the whole class.

> **Answers**
> I would like to place an order for 2,000 motherboards. This is a repeat order. We need these urgently so please send them asap. Please charge it to our account as usual.

Exercise 3

▶ **9.4** Students work in pairs. Before they listen, ask them to imagine how Gisele is feeling after the two-week delay. Was the equipment needed urgently? (Yes). How would they feel in the situation? What would they want to know?

Ask students to read the supplier's information to know what to listen for. Play the listening. Let students compare their answers with a partner. Check answers in whole-class feedback.

> **Answers**
> Account: Abracomp
> Account reference: PG 278
> Date of order: 11 February
> Product description: motherboards
> Quantity: 2,000
> Dispatched: Yes
> Date and time dispatched: the afternoon of the 11th

Exercise 4

▶ **9.4** Students work in pairs. Tell them to read the sentence halves and match 1–8 and a–h to make complete sentences. Play the listening for them to check their answers. If necessary, stop after each sentence and elicit the answer.

> **Answers**
> 1 f 2 e 3 g 4 c 5 a 6 d 7 h 8 b

EXTENSION Remind students that to clarify spelling we can use common words (names, cities, countries) to illustrate a letter: *That's P for Peter.*
For easily confused numbers, for example, 18 and 80, you can say each digit after the number: *The number is 18 – one, eight.*
Ask students to spell their names, give dates and numbers using the clarifications for practice.

Further practice

If students need more practice, go to *Practice file 9* on page 122 of the *Student's Book*.

Exercise 5

Students work in pairs. Student A turns to page 139, and B to page 143. They take turns to role-play the situations on the phone. Give students time to read the information and prepare the questions and answers for each of their situations. Refer them to the *Key expressions*. If possible, have the students sit back to back so they can't see each other. Give them a time limit for each situation. You could give them a signal to change situations. Monitor, checking they are using the language from the *Key expressions*. Provide whole-class feedback by asking two or three pairs to act out their phone calls.

Photocopiable worksheet

Download and photocopy *Unit 9 Business communication worksheet* from the teacher resources in the *Online practice*.

Talking point

Discussion

Exercise 1

Ask students to look at the pictures and the title of the article. What do they think shadow work is? Ask the class for ideas. Then tell students to read the article and answer the questions. Ask two or three students for their ideas.

PRE-WORK LEARNERS Ask students to think about their college or university. Are there occasions where they think they have to do / find out things for themself that might in the past have been provided by their teachers? What advantages and disadvantages can they think of for working more independently?

Exercise 2

Ask students to discuss the advantages and disadvantages of shadow work for businesses with a partner. Check answers by asking one or two pairs for their ideas.

> **Possible answer**
> Shadow work may reduce a business's costs but it may also put off customers who prefer more traditional customer service.

Exercise 3

Ask students to discuss the questions with a partner. Check answers by asking one or two pairs for their ideas. You could continue with questions: Can they think of other examples of shadow work? How will shadow work increase in the future?

> **Possible answer**
> Some people might enjoy doing shadow work such as browsing for products online or being in charge of their own shopping because it makes them feel they are saving time rather than losing free-time.

Task

Exercise 1

Ask each student in the class to think about their own company or business and make a list of the different jobs involved in producing their goods or offering their services.

`PRE-WORK LEARNERS` Ask students to work in pairs and find out about a (real) business from the Internet. They should then make a list of the jobs involved in running this business.

Exercise 2

Give students time to think about how they can make some of the jobs on their lists into shadow work, and what the benefits to the company could be.

Exercise 3

Students work in pairs, taking turns to present their company's goods and services and the ideas they have about shadow work to each other.

Provide whole-class feedback by asking two or three pairs to give their presentations. Then ask the class how they think the customers and clients would feel if the jobs became shadow work? How would the staff in the company feel?

`PRE-WORK LEARNERS` Put students in small groups and ask them to imagine they work for a (real) company or business. They make a list of the different jobs involved in producing the company's goods or offering its service. Each small group can take a different company. They could look up the information about the company they choose on the Internet.
Give students time to think about how they can make some of the jobs on their lists into shadow work and how that could benefit the company.
Now pair students from different groups so they can take turns to present their company's goods and services and the ideas they have about shadow work to each other.

`ONE-TO-ONE` Ask the student to think about his/her business and make a list of the different jobs involved in producing its goods or offering its service. Then he/she decides what jobs can be made into shadow jobs and how that would benefit the company.

Progress test

Download and photocopy *Unit 9 Progress test* and *Speaking test* from the teacher resources in the *Online practice*.

Viewpoint 3

Preview

The topic of this *Viewpoint* is *Cybercrime*. In this *Viewpoint*, students begin by watching and discussing a video of six people talking about computer problems and how these problems were solved. Students then watch and discuss an interview with Fraser Howard, a principle threat researcher at Sophos, a leading Internet security firm. Finally, the students do a task which involves writing a summary of the main points raised in the interview.

Exercise 1

Allow students time to look at the list of problems. Then ask them to discuss the list with a partner. You could ask them how they resolved the problems.

Exercise 2

▶ **01** Make sure students look at the questions in the table before watching the video. Play the video and ask students to take notes. If necessary, pause after each speaker to allow writing time.

Answers

	What was the problem?	How did they solve the problem?
Speaker 1	couldn't transfer music onto daughter's MP3 player; computer software didn't recognize the device	followed instructions; disconnected and switched off MP3 player; cleaned connections; turned off computer and plugged it back in again
Speaker 2	strength of wi-fi connection in classrooms	not solved; still a problem
Speaker 3	unable to open a program; lost a document	looked in folders; tweaked settings; raised a call with the IT Help Desk who solved the problem
Speaker 4	accessing the network; logging onto PC; programs not running correctly	call Help Desk in Romania for a solution or to fix the problem remotely
Speaker 5	one of laptop screens stopped working; didn't turn on	tried to move lots of wires; phoned IT department who fixed it
Speaker 6	computer shutting down unexpectedly	getting a new computer

Exercise 3

Ask students to compare their answers to **2** with a partner. Did the people in the video have the same problems as them in **1**?

Exercise 4

Before they watch the video, ask students to read the sentences and replace the words in bold with words from the list. Then ask them to compare their answers with a partner. You could check that students understand the meaning of *anonymously* and *target*.

For further practice, ask students to work in pairs and take turns to say a word and give the synonym. You could also ask them to write a sentence for each of the words in the list for homework.

Answers

1 secure	**5** redirects
2 tricks	**6** adapts
3 gets into	**7** installs
4 browses	**8** steals

Exercise 5

▶ **02** Ask students to read the scenes A–E from the video. To focus students on the video images only, you could turn the sound off so students just watch for and number the scenes.

Tell students to number the scenes in the correct order 1–5 as they watch. Check answers in whole-class feedback.

Answers

A 3 **B** 5 **C** 4 **D** 1 **E** 2

VIDEO SCRIPT

Part 1

Technology has always been used by criminals and the Internet – where people can operate anonymously all over the world – is the perfect tool. We now live in the age of cybercrime.
This is Fraser Howard. He is a principle threat researcher at Sophos, one of the world's leading Internet security firms.

What is cybercrime?

Cybercrime is fundamentally crime but specifically using computers or the Internet to deliver the attack.
Internet security is basically the steps taken to protect yourself from online attacks.
Internet security is necessary because criminals are targeting users, targeting businesses, looking to steal data in order to profit financially from internet attacks.

Part 2

Today almost everybody has been a victim of some kind of cybercrime. But how exactly does it happen? Here, Fraser talks us through an example of cybercrime.

How does cybercrime happen?

Most people today get infected as they're browsing the web. So, as they're browsing around they come across a site, a real website, but one that might have been hacked by hackers in order to redirect their browser to somewhere bad; bad stuff happens and their machine gets infected. And that's what we have in this video here.
As the real web page loads, there's nothing that the user can see that tells them anything is going wrong. But as the page loads, in the background bad stuff is happening and their machine is becoming infected with malware.
So, after a second or so this application, calling itself Security Shield, is now installed on the system, and this is the malware. And it's going to

run; it's going to tell them they have lots of problems on their system; and it's going to try, try to trick the user into paying for removal of these non-existent problems.

Part 3
Where did this example of cybercrime happen?
We can look at that exact attack from a geographical perspective to get a bit more idea of how it's constructed. We start off in the UK, which is where we're browsing the website from, and that first real site that we're browsing to is hosted on a server in Vancouver, Canada. As I said, this is a real site; a normal company site, but one that happens to have been hacked by hackers in order to redirect to somewhere bad. So, it causes your browser to redirect to a server in Russia. This server in Russia then bounces your browser onto another server, this time one in the United States.

Part 4
How is cybercrime changing?
One of the ways in which cybercrime is changing is the target, the actual data that the criminals are after is, is changing in form. Rather than just being focused on information stored on a computer, we're now looking at information stored on mobile devices. There's a broader range of attacks that therefore become possible. And when we think about security and how we secure our information we're not just looking at securing computers we're looking at securing our home networks, our mobile phones, our tablets.
To respond to the changes in cybercrime and the types of attacks that the criminals are using Internet security also has to continually adapt. And so Internet security nowadays provides solutions that aren't just focused on your computer; they're focused on your entire business network or even your home network, across multiple devices, multiple computers.

Exercise 6
▶ **03** Ask students to read the two parts of the sentences and try to match them. Then play Part 1 of the video for them to check their answers. Check answers in whole-class feedback.

Answers
1 c 2 b 3 a

Exercise 7
▶ **04** Ask students to read sentences A–F carefully. Ask them to think about the order they expect them to come in. Let students check their answers with a partner. Play Part 2 of the video and tell them to check their ideas as they watch. Check answers in whole-class feedback.

Answers
A 6 B 1 C 2 D 4 E 5 F 3

Exercise 8
▶ **05** Ask students to read the questions and see if they remember any of the answers. Play Part 3 of the video. Check answers in whole-class feedback.

Answers
1 The UK	3 Russia
2 Vancouver, Canada	4 A server in the USA

Exercise 9
▶ **06** Ask students to read the summary sentences carefully. Play Part 4 of the video. Ask students to decide with a partner which summary is best. Ask them to give reasons for their choice. Check answers in whole-class feedback.

Answer
B

ONE-TO-ONE Ask the student which computer problems he/she has encountered at work. How does his/her company resolve problems? Does it have outside consultants helping, or an internal IT department?

Exercise 10
Ask students to work in pairs and to use the words in the word cloud to summarize the interview. Tell them to make sure they use all of the words.

Exercise 11
Each student then writes his/her own summary. Remind them of the word limit of 100–120 words, and that they should use all the words in **10**. Then they should try to make their sentences flow by joining the sentences using the words *because, however, although,* etc.

When they have completed their summaries, students can watch video **02** again to check how accurate their summary is. You could also ask each student to swap their summaries with another student and compare what they have written.

EXTENSION It might be a good idea here to run through with students how to write a good summary.
Only write the key points; leave out the details. Don't quote the original speaker. Use your own words, paraphrase what you have heard, replacing words and phrases with synonyms. It can be necessary to change the original grammatical structure, for example, *Changing your password every month can prevent hackers stealing your data.* = *Changing your password regularly secures your data.*
Join sentences using linking words and relative pronouns like *because, as, however, although, despite, which, who,* etc. Write a draft and then go back to check you have included all the key points.

Further video ideas
You can find a list of suggested ideas for how to use video in the class in the teacher resources in the *Online practice*.

10 Facilities

Unit content

By the end of this unit, students will be able to
- describe a place of work and its facilities
- use quantifiers
- use *too* and *enough*
- make suggestions and recommendations.

Context

The topic of *Facilities* gives students the language to describe and evaluate this very important feature of the workplace, including its staff facilities. In any business, it is essential to have systems to motivate the company staff, to let them feel that the company not only values their work, but appreciates them as people. To do this, learners cover the language needed to describe staff facilities and compare and contrast different facilities. They also evaluate the concept of generating new ideas, which are often developed in technology companies to encourage creativity and openness among employees.

It is important to follow national and local rules and regulations, regarding health and safety in the workplace. To do this, students study quantifiers, countable and uncountable nouns, and *too* and *enough*, to make their descriptions of the workplace more accurate.

In this unit, students will also learn how to make suggestions and respond to them in a business setting. They will have the opportunity to role-play a situation as an employer and a health and safety inspector discussing facilities and their importance for the staff.

In the *Talking point*, students will have the opportunity to examine motivation and the 'Hawthorne Effect'. They will discuss what it is and the effect it has on efficiency and performance. They will then work out what they consider to be the most successful motivational factors. Finally, they will read about a real-life experiment on motivation in business, carried out by the American psychologist Frederick Herzberg, and discuss its relevance to their own experiences.

Starting point

Do the first question with the whole class. Give them cues if they are hesitant: *in an office, factory, school*, etc. The second question can be done with the whole class or in pairs before whole-class feedback. Encourage students to develop their answers.

Possible answers
1 office, factory, school, bank, shop, airport, construction site, garage, law courts, transport: buses, trains, lorries, etc.

Working with words

Exercise 1

Ask students to discuss the questions with a partner. Ask two or three pairs for their suggestions in whole class feedback.

Exercise 2

Ask students to look at the questions and read the article. They can then discuss the answers with a partner. Tell students it's not necessary to understand all the words at this stage, only the general sense. Check they understand the words in the glossary, as they are important to the general understanding of the article. Provide feedback on answers with the whole class.

Answers
1 By knocking down the walls and getting rid of old-fashioned office furniture.
2 Video-conferencing, breakout areas, open-plan spaces, corridors with whiteboards, a presentation suite, a gym, a games room and a music room.
3 It's good for different types of meetings, it encourages creativity and openness, and makes chance interactions more likely which often lead to great ideas. It also helps to make work stress-free and keeps employees 'at the top of their game'.

Exercise 3

Ask students to work in pairs and compare the facilities at their workplace with Google's. Then they can come up with a list of five facilities they would like to have and what the benefits of the facilities would be. Ask them to join with another pair and compare their lists, then choose three facilities as a group. Ask two or three groups to tell the whole class what is on their list, and why they chose these facilities, to provide whole-class feedback.

PRE-WORK LEARNERS Ask students to imagine they work for a company which is planning to update its facilities. In small groups, they come up with a list of five facilities they think a modern company should have and what the benefits would be. Then ask two groups to work together and come up with the three facilities that all twenty-first century companies should have. Ask them to explain their choices. Provide whole-class feedback by asking the groups to read out their lists and explain their choices.

Exercise 4

Ask students to read the article in **2** again quickly and match the words in bold to the definitions 1–9. Remind students that one answer matches two adjectives. Let students compare answers with a partner. Check answers in whole-class feedback.

Answers
1 old-fashioned
2 hi-tech, state-of-the-art
3 open-plan
4 spacious
5 stress-free
6 comfortable
7 futuristic
8 fun
9 fully-equipped

Exercise 5

Students work in pairs. Ask them to take turns to describe their place of work to their partner. You could set it up as an interview by giving each student a few minutes to prepare their questions and answers using some of the word prompts, and the adjectives in **4**, to describe their workplace. Students then interview each other, and perhaps take some notes to report back to the class.

Provide whole-class feedback by asking three or four students to describe their partner's workplace.

PRE-WORK LEARNERS Ask groups of students to find information on the Internet about the facilities for staff provided by different well-known companies, for example, Apple, Starbucks, Marks & Spencer, Harrods, etc., or famous companies in their country. Each group can then present information about each of their companies to the whole class. The class as a whole can decide which of them offers the most attractive facilities.

Exercise 6

▶ **10.1** Tell students they are going to listen to two people discussing workspaces and facilities. Ask them to write down the adjectives the people use to describe these. Play the listening and tell students to check their answers with a partner. Check answers in whole-class feedback. If necessary, play the listening again, pausing for students to write down the adjectives.

Answers
Speaker 1: spacious, hi-tech, relaxing
Speaker 2: state-of-the-art, old-fashioned, (not) up-to-date, stress-free

Exercise 7

Students work in pairs. Tell them to look at the answers in **6** and think about the adverbs that the speakers used with them. Students write the adverbs in the correct place on the scale. Check answers in whole-class feedback.

Answers
not very, not exactly, fairly, pretty, really, very, extremely

Exercise 8

▶ **10.1** Tell students to listen and match the adverbs to the adjectives. Play the listening again. You could ask them to

practise saying the adverb + adjective combinations, making sure they use the correct word stress.

Answers
1 really spacious
2 very hi-tech
3 extremely relaxing
4 not exactly state-of-the-art
5 fairly old-fashioned
6 not very up-to-date
7 pretty stress-free

EXTENSION You could ask students to write sentences for each of the adverb + adjective combinations that are true for them, e.g. *My new office is really spacious. The one I worked in before was much smaller, and I had to share it with seven other people.* They then take turns reading them to a partner, giving reasons for their ideas.

Further practice

If students need more practice, go to *Practice file 10* on page 124 of the *Student's Book*.

Exercise 9

Students work in pairs and follow the instructions. Give students time to think about the different places and how they are going to describe them. Refer students to the *Tip*. You could check they understand the uses by asking them to come up with an example for each use of *like*. Give them a time limit. Students then take turns describing each prompt. Provide whole-class feedback by asking two or three students to report back to the class.

PRE-WORK LEARNERS You could ask students to describe their ideal place to work for the first prompt, and a part of their school or college they don't like so much for the third prompt.

Exercise 10

Tell students to work in pairs and turn to page 140 and follow the instructions. Give them time to choose the place they are going to describe and prepare how they are going to describe it. Remind them not to give the name of the place they are describing. Monitor, checking they are using the adverbs and adjectives correctly.

For feedback, ask three students to describe three different places and the class to guess which one they are describing.

Photocopiable worksheet

Download and photocopy *Unit 10 Working with words worksheet* from the teacher resources in the *Online practice*.

Language at work

Exercise 1

Ask students to discuss the question with a partner. Ask one or two pairs to give feedback to the whole class.

PRE-WORK LEARNERS Ask students about the health and safety rules at their school or college. Do they know what they are? How can they find out about them? Do they think they help protect students? If so, how? If not, how should they be improved?

Exercise 2

Tell students to read the information leaflet and add the headings. Let them compare answers with a partner. Check the answers in whole-class feedback.

Answers
1 Welfare
2 Health
3 Safety

Exercise 3

▶ 10.2 Tell students to quickly read the information leaflet in **2** again. Play the listening. Students tick the items in the leaflet the inspector and employer discuss. Students compare answers with a partner and then do whole-class feedback.

Answers
Conversation 1: A place to store clothing
Conversation 2: Somewhere to take breaks, windows in all rooms, suitable lighting

Exercise 4

▶ 10.2 Ask students to read the sentences and complete them with the quantifiers. Let students compare answers with a partner. Play the listening again for them to check the answers.

Answers
1 A lot of
2 many
3 much
4 some
5 any
6 a few
7 not many
8 any
9 a little

Exercise 5

Ask students to read the answers in **4** and choose the correct category for the nouns in the sentences. They check answers with a partner, before whole-class feedback.

Answers
1 employees, people, lockers, places, chairs, windows
2 space, staff, paint

Exercise 6

Students choose the correct option from the sentences in **4** to complete the *Language point*. They check answers with a partner, before whole-class feedback.

Answers
1 a lot of, any, a few
2 some, much, a lot of, any, a little
3 a few, a little, not many, not much
4 a lot of, many, much
5 many, much, any
6 not any, not many, not much, not a lot of

Grammar reference

If students need more information, go to *Grammar reference* on page 125 of the *Student's Book*.

Exercise 7

Ask students to underline the correct option, reminding them that in one sentence both options are correct. They compare answers with a partner and then check answers in whole-class feedback.

Answers
1 much
2 a lot of
3 any
4 A few
5 any
6 some
7 a little
8 many / a lot of

Further practice

If students need more practice, go to *Practice file 10* on page 125 of the *Student's Book*.

Exercise 8

Tell students to work in pairs, taking turns to ask and answer questions about the prompts. Give students a few minutes to prepare the questions and the descriptions of the facilities for staff in their workplaces.

If all the students are from the same company, then ask them to look up two real, well-known companies on the Internet. The students prepare the information for the company they have chosen using the prompts, inventing the answers if necessary.

They take turns to ask and answer the questions about the facilities in each company. To provide whole-class feedback, ask two or three pairs to ask and answer the questions for the class.

PRE-WORK LEARNERS Put students in two groups, group A and group B. Tell the groups that they are going to role-play an employer and a health and safety inspector. The inspector is inspecting a company. Ask group A to imagine they are each the health and safety inspector and to prepare the questions for the task. Ask group B to imagine they are each an employer and to think about what the inspectors will ask about so they can give the inspector the information he/she needs.

Now put the students in AB pairs. They then ask and answer the questions. Provide whole-class feedback by asking two or three pairs to ask and answer the questions for the class.

Photocopiable worksheet

Download and photocopy *Unit 10 Language at work worksheet* from the teacher resources in the *Online practice*.

Practically speaking

Exercise 1

▶ 10.3 Start by explaining the situation and asking students to listen and answer the questions. Play the listening. Check answers in whole-class feedback.

Answers
They are discussing the employees' room for breaks and storing belongings.
1 enough
2 enough
3 too
4 too

Exercise 2

Ask students to read the sentences in **1** and complete the categories. Let them compare answers with a partner. Check answers in whole-class feedback.

Answers
a too
b enough
c too
d enough

Exercise 3

Students work in pairs. Ask them to read the situations and then describe each one using *too* and *enough*. Check answers in whole-class feedback.

Suggested answers
The memory is too small. / The memory isn't big enough.
The sun is too bright.
It's too cold. / It isn't warm enough.
The staff don't have enough work. / They have too little work.
There's enough space. / The storeroom is big enough.

Exercise 4

Ask students to make three sentences about their company facilities using *too* and *enough* and then take turns to tell a partner. Provide whole-class feedback by asking two or three pairs to describe their partner's workplace facilities for the class.

PRE-WORK LEARNERS Ask students to make three sentences about the facilities at their school or college using *too* and *enough*. They take turns to tell their partner.

Business communication

Exercise 1

Ask students how suggestions are made in their company. Check answers in whole-class feedback.

PRE-WORK LEARNERS Ask students to think about what the most successful ways to make suggestions might be in 1) a small company and 2) a very large company. Ask them to give reasons for their choices. Check answers in whole-class feedback.

Exercise 2

Ask students to read the comments from the suggestion box and complete them with the expressions. Check answers with the whole class.

Answers
1 why don't
2 we could always
3 have you thought about
4 Couldn't we do

Exercise 3

▶ 10.4 Students work in pairs. Before they listen, ask them to read the suggestions in **2** again quickly. Ask students to read the questions to know what to listen for. Play the listening. Let students compare their answers with a partner. Check answers in whole-class feedback.

Answers
1 There isn't enough space for both ideas.
2 They choose the crèche because employees might spend too long in the relaxation area.

Exercise 4

Ask students to read the sentences and choose the correct option. Check answers with a partner before whole-class feedback.

Answers
1 difficult
2 having
3 reservations
4 better
5 have
6 putting

Exercise 5

▶ 10.4 Students listen and tick the responses they hear. Play the listening again. Check answers, pausing the listening to elicit the answers, if necessary.

Answers
I really like it.
Good idea.
Sorry, but I don't think that would work.
Great!
Exactly.

EXTENSION You could ask students to practise by making very short two-line conversations using the expressions in **4** and **5**, where they take turns making and responding to suggestions, for example:

A *I think we should consider buying new laptops for everyone.*
B *I'm not sure. We need to be careful about our budget this year.*

Further practice

If students need more practice, go to *Practice file 10* on page 124 of the *Student's Book*.

Exercise 6

Students work in pairs. Ask them to turn to page 140 and follow the instructions. Refer students to the *Key expressions* to help them. Give students a time limit to prepare their ideas and come up with their recommendations. They then try to agree on a style for the office space.

ONE-TO-ONE Ask the student to turn to page 140 and choose the style he/she prefers and to present his/her ideas to you. You put the argument for the other style. You both then try to persuade each other to change their mind.

Exercise 7

Put students in small groups and, remembering what they decided in **6,** ask them to come up with their suggestions for an Anarchy Zone, giving a good reason for each one. Once the group has decided on the four items, they prepare a short presentation giving their recommendations to the whole class. Those listening should think of questions about the suggestions, or reasons why the suggestions are good or not.

You could finish by getting the class to come up with a final class list of four items, and the reasons why these are the best choices.

ONE-TO-ONE Ask the student to think about his/her own company. Does he/she think something like an Anarchy Zone or Relaxation Room would work for it? Ask him/her to think of at least two arguments for, and two against, either the Anarchy Zone or Relaxation Room. He/she presents the arguments and finally decides on whether to have the new area.

Photocopiable worksheet

Download and photocopy *Unit 10 Business communication worksheet* from the teacher resources in the *Online practice.*

Talking point

Discussion

Exercise 1

Ask students to read the article on the 'Hawthorne Effect' and answer the question, reminding them to give reasons. Ask two or three students for their ideas.

> **Possible answers**
> Yes, this finding is true, we are always more motivated when we think someone is interested in us.
> No, we are able to motivate ourselves if the work is interesting enough.

Exercise 2

Ask students work in small groups and make a list of five factors that motivate people. Ask them to give reasons for their choices. Check answers by asking one or two groups to feed back to the whole class.

Exercise 3

Ask students to discuss the questions with a partner. Check answers by asking one or two pairs for their ideas.

PRE-WORK LEARNERS Put students in small groups and ask them to come up with four or five ways to motivate students to improve their performance.

Task

Exercise 1

Put students in small groups and tell them to follow the instructions. Remind them they only have 30 points to share

among the items and that they should agree how the points are shared, as a group. You may want to give them a time limit for this part of the task.

ONE-TO-ONE Ask the student to look at the list of motivating factors. Ask him/her to decide what the top six factors are and explain why. Ask him/her to decide which factors are not important, if any, and to explain why. You could ask him/her which factors he/she thinks have had the most effect on his/her own motivation at work.

Exercise 2

Regroup the students, putting one or two from each group into a new group. They then compare their results and justify their scores.

Exercise 3

Explain to students that this task is based on a real experiment. Tell them to turn to page 141 and read about Frederick Herzberg's research and findings. Ask students if they agree and if their findings were similar to Herzberg's. Ask them to decide what the experiment shows about motivating people at work and if they think Herzberg's findings apply to them.

Progress test

Download and photocopy *Unit 10 Progress test* and *Speaking test* from the teacher resources in the *Online practice.*

11 Decisions

Unit content

By the end of this unit, students will be able to

- talk about decision-making
- talk about future possibilities
- use *if* in different ways
- negotiate an agreement.

Context

The topic of *Decisions* gives students the language to discuss how we consider possibilities and make decisions. In any business it is essential to make good decisions and to communicate them effectively to colleagues and customers. To do this, learners cover the language needed to describe, prioritize, evaluate and reach a decision. They look at how decision-making works in a real company, and the innovative approach the company has for including more employees than just the managers in the process.

It is important to be able to express future possibilities when prioritizing and evaluating decisions. To do this, students will cover the first conditional form to express possible future situations and the second conditional form to express improbable and hypothetical situations. They will look at various expressions which use *if*.

In this unit, students will also learn how to negotiate in a business setting. They will have the opportunity to look at how negotiations are structured and the language to make suggestions and respond to them in a negotiation situation.

In the *Talking point*, the students will play a game where they discuss various situations and possible outcomes in order to use first and second conditionals in a natural setting.

Starting point

Do the first question in small groups to start with, and then with the whole class. Ask students to read the four statements and decide which one describes them best. They compare answers in their groups and then the group says which statement most students agreed with. Encourage students to develop their answers. The second question can be done in pairs before whole-class feedback, but you may find the worst decision a sensitive topic and want to avoid it.

Working with words

Exercise 1

Allow students a few minutes to think about the question and then ask them to discuss their ideas with a partner.

Exercise 2

▶ 11.1 Ask students to look at 'The Priority Matrix' and listen to a trainer explaining its four parts. Make sure they understand what *urgent* means, i.e. not only that the action is important, but that it has to be done <u>very quickly</u>. While they listen, they number each part as they hear it discussed. Play the listening. Students can then discuss the answers with a partner. Provide feedback on answers with the whole class. If necessary, play the listening again, pausing to elicit the answers.

Answers
1 Do now (or do it quickly)
2 Think and plan
3 Delegate
4 Ignore

Exercise 3

Ask students to work in pairs and read the four tasks a–d. Then they put them into the matrix in **2**. Ask them to give reasons for their answers. Ask them to join with another pair and compare their ideas. Provide feedback on answers with the whole class, checking why they chose the answers.

Suggested answers
a **Think and plan** because it's important but it is 12 months away.
b **Delegate** because it's important to recognize the employee but it's probably something that somebody else can do.
c **Do now** because you don't want to lose this customer so you need to solve the problem immediately.
d **Ignore** because it isn't a priority and you have much more important things to deal with.

Exercise 4

Give students time to think about four or five jobs they have to do and where they can put them on the matrix.

Exercise 5

Ask students to take turns to talk about their decisions from **4** with a partner. Make sure they discuss how useful the Priority Matrix was in their decision-making. Provide whole-class feedback by asking three or four students to describe one of their partner's decisions, where it was on the matrix and why their partner placed it there.

ONE-TO-ONE Ask the student to make a list of four or five jobs he/she has to do and put them on the matrix. Ask them to explain their rationale to you. Then ask him/her to evaluate the Matrix – *How useful is it to their situation? How to they prioritize? Do they use something like this? If not, what do they do?*

Exercise 6

▶ 11.1 Tell students to read sentences 1–8 and replace the words in bold with the verbs from the list. They can check their answers with a partner. Play listening **11.1** again and tell them to check their answers. Check answers in whole-class feedback. If necessary, play the listening again, pausing for students to write down the verbs.

Answers
2 prioritize
3 reach
4 invite
5 evaluate
6 delegate
7 avoid
8 ignore

Exercise 7

Tell students to complete the article about decision-making at Suma with six of the answers in **6**. Let them check their answers with a partner. Check answers in whole-class feedback.

Answers
1 reach
2 invited
3 ignored
4 avoid
5 prioritize
6 delegated

Exercise 8

Students work in pairs. Tell them to match the words in bold in the article in **7** with the definitions 1–7. Check answers in whole-class feedback. Make sure students can pronounce the words with the correct stress.

Answers
1 consul<u>ta</u>tion
2 confron<u>ta</u>tion
3 hier<u>ar</u>chical
4 demo<u>cra</u>tic
5 <u>mem</u>ber
6 con<u>sen</u>sus
7 co<u>op</u>erative

Further practice

If students need more practice, go to *Practice file 11* on page 126 of the *Student's Book*.

Exercise 9

Students work in two groups, A and B, and follow the instructions. Give students time to think about their list and the reasons for their choices. You could give them a time limit.

If the class is large, you could have several groups – As and Bs – so that everyone has a chance to take part.

Tell students they are going to present their lists and give them time to prepare the presentation. To keep this moving, give each group a time limit for their presentation.

ONE-TO-ONE Ask the student to make a list of advantages and disadvantages of decision-making with a cooperative like Suma. Ask him/her to give reasons for his/her choices, and to decide whether he/she thinks this is a good way of decision-making.

Possible answers
Group A
Advantages in cooperatives:
Everyone is involved in the process
Employees feel more motivated and take responsibility
Decisions are made based on more viewpoints so all outcomes can be anticipated
Disadvantages in hierarchical structures:
Only a few people are involved
People wait for others to make decisions
Hierarchies often slow down decision-making

Group B
Disadvantages of decision-making with a cooperative:
Impossible to include everyone's views
One person will eventually have to decide
Not everyone has the knowledge to comment on every aspect of the business
Time-consuming to get everyone's view
Advantages in more hierarchical structures:
People who are more qualified and experienced make the key decisions
Better to have only a few people focussed on strategic thinking
If well-organized it can be faster than waiting to build a consensus.

Exercise 10

Each group presents its list of advantages and disadvantages, giving its rationale for the points included. If there is more than one group A and B, they can take turns to present. Those listening should ask questions to clarify points. If necessary, ask students the reason each point is on the list.

Either have a whole-class discussion on the different views to reach a consensus on the best approach to decision-making, or make smaller groups, one A and B, for the discussion phase. Then each group A and B can present its consensus to the whole group.

ONE-TO-ONE Ask the student to present his/her ideas to you. Then ask him/her to compare the Suma process with his/her own company. Does he/she think the company could improve decision-making using Suma's methods? Why/Why not? Does he/she think Suma's methods would work in different cultures? Why/Why not?

Photocopiable worksheet
Download and photocopy *Unit 11 Working with words worksheet* from the teacher resources in the *Online practice*.

Language at work

Exercise 1
Ask students to discuss the questions with a partner. Ask one or two pairs to give feedback to the whole class.

Exercise 2
Tell students to read the email and answer the questions. Let them compare answers with a partner. Check the answers in whole-class feedback.

Answer
Ilse has to decide whether to relocate to a new out-of-town shopping centre. Her options are move or stay at her current town-centre location. Jeff may tell her to stay where she is, as they have an established customer base.

Exercise 3
Tell students to read the email in **2** again quickly and, in the *Language point*, match the sentences a–c to the two types of conditionals. Students compare answers with a partner and then do whole-class feedback.

Answers
a 1 b 1 c 2

Grammar reference
If students need more information, go to *Grammar reference* on page 127 of the *Student's Book*.

Exercise 4
Refer students to the *Tip*. Ask them to read the sentences and choose the correct option. Let students compare answers with a partner. Check the answers in whole-class feedback, eliciting the reason for the correct answer.

Answers

1 wouldn't	5 Unless
2 're	6 Will
3 want	7 would
4 had	

Further practice
If students need more practice, go to *Practice file 11* on page 127 of the *Student's Book*.

Exercise 5
Tell students to read sentences 1–8 and complete them with their own words and ideas.

Possible answers
2 you might miss out on a great opportunity
3 I come up with a good idea
4 won't benefit from their knowledge
5 wouldn't have time to manage
6 'll fail to lead
7 people won't compromise
8 'd probably take it and travel for a year

Exercise 6
Students work in pairs. They take turns to read out their sentences in **5**. They can compare ideas with their partner and check the verb forms are correct. Monitor, checking students are using the correct verb forms.

Exercise 7
Ask students to work in pairs, or in small groups. Give them time to think of the answers to the questions and the correct verb forms to use. They can then take turns discussing the questions and comparing answers. Monitor, checking they are using the correct verb forms.

PRE-WORK LEARNERS Ask students to imagine they work for a big international company and answer the questions. You could ask students to check out well-known companies on the Internet, such as Starbucks, Amazon or Microsoft, so they have an idea of where they might possibly relocate to and who their main competitors are.

Photocopiable worksheet
Download and photocopy *Unit 11 Language at work worksheet* from the teacher resources in the *Online practice*.

Practically speaking

Exercise 1
▶ 11.2 Ask students to read the questions. Explain that they are going to listen to four conversations and answer the questions. Play the listening. Check answers in whole-class feedback, pausing the listening to elicit the answers if necessary.

Answers
1 The decision is difficult. The other person doesn't agree.
2 The deadline is the end of the week. They don't have time and money.
3 A meeting is starting. Walter's appointment is at the doctor's.
4 The increase in the cost is 20%.

Exercise 2
▶ 11.2 Ask students to match sentences a–d with the conversations in **1**. Let them compare answers with a partner. Play the listening again. Students listen and check answers in whole-class feedback. Make sure the students note the grammatical structures and functions in the phrases:
What if + present or past tense
form: *what if* + present tense – 1st conditional – possible/probable suggestion
what if + past tense – 2nd conditional – improbable

suggestion/unlikely to happen
function: suggestion

If I were (was) you + would
form: 2nd conditional – hypothetical/impossible situation,
(*If I were you* is a set phrase for advice; *If I was you* is a
common acceptable spoken form for advice)
function: advice

If you don't mind + future or would like
form: *If* + present tense (semi-fixed expression) – checking
listener's attitude
function: requesting permission

If only + past tense
form: *If only* + past tense – fixed expression
function: expressing regret about a present situation

Answers
a Conversation 4
b Conversation 1
c Conversation 3
d Conversation 2

Exercise 3

Ask students to read the words and expressions in bold in **2**
and then match the *if* expression with the meanings. Check
answers in whole-class feedback.

Answers
Giving advice: *If I were you* …
Suggesting: *What if* …?
Wishing: *If only* …
Making a request: *If you don't mind* …

PRONUNCIATION Ask students to listen again, and listen
to how the phrases in **2** are said. Ask them to listen for the
intonation on the four *if* phrases and practise it. Point out
how the intonation changes for giving advice, suggesting,
wishing or making a request.
Then tell them to work in pairs and write a short three- or
four-line conversation for each phrase. They take turns
practising the conversations so each student says the *if*
phrase. Monitor, making sure they are using the correct
intonation for each situation.

Exercise 4

Ask students to work in pairs. Tell them to follow the
instructions.
Provide whole-class feedback by asking two or three pairs to
report what they said for each situation.

PRE-WORK LEANERS Ask students to give their partner
advice about their studies for the first prompt, for example,
what they should study, if they should change their studies,
how hard they should work; and to wish for something
to improve in their academic life for the third prompt. For
the fourth prompt, they can request permission from their
teacher to miss class.

EXTENSION Ask students to work in small groups. They
discuss the following dilemmas and come up with a
suggestion or some advice:
1 You find $100 in the street.
2 You forget to send an important document to a client on
   time or hand in an essay to your tutor by the deadline.
   They are now very angry about it arriving late.

3 You oversleep and so miss an important appointment
   with a client or miss an exam.
4 You are offered a great job but it means you have to move
   to another country.
5 A friend asks to borrow $50. You know he/she needs
   the money, but you also know they probably won't pay
   you back.

Business communication

Exercise 1

Ask students to discuss the situations with a partner. Check
answers in whole-class feedback by asking two or three
students to report back.

PRE-WORK LEARNERS Ask students to think about difficult
situations and when they have had to negotiate with other
people; for example:

* agreeing with a member of your family what colour to
   paint the living room or kitchen
* deciding who will pay for a meal out when you are with
   friends
* asking your teacher for time off before an important exam
* discussing with family/a friend which film to see.

Check answers in whole-class feedback.

Exercise 2

▶ **11.3** Explain to students that they are going to listen
to part of a conversation. Patricia, who works for a UK
manufacturing company, is negotiating with Laszlo, who is a
distributor in Hungary. Ask students to read the questions to
know what to listen for. Play the listening. Let students check
their answers with a partner. Check answers with the whole
class.

Answers
1 Three years.
2 The brand is virtually unknown in Hungary so it will take time
   to build a customer base.
3 So it is linked to performance with an option to end the
   contract.
4 Because they don't try to compromise.

Exercise 3

▶ **11.4** Students work in pairs. Before they listen, ask them
to read the negotiation stages. Ask students to listen and
tick which of the stages they hear being discussed. Play the
listening. Let students compare their answers with a partner.
Check answers in whole-class feedback. You could let the
students go to the audio script on page 154 of the *Student's
Book* to find the useful expressions, as they follow the early
stages of the negotiation.

Answers
Students hear all the stages of the negotiation.

Exercise 4

▶ **11.4** Tell students to read the expressions before they
listen. They number the expressions in the order they hear
them. Let students compare their answers with a partner.
Play the listening again. Check answers in whole-class
feedback.

Further practice

If students need more practice, go to *Practice file 11* on page 126 of the *Student's Book*.

Exercise 5

Students work in pairs to practise negotiating. Student A starts the negotiations and Student B responds. Refer students to the *Key expressions* to help them do the negotiating. Tell students to follow the conversation instructions. They then swap roles and repeat the negotiation.

Monitor, checking they are using the expressions correctly.

Exercise 6

Ask students to turn to their relevant page. Student A turns to page 141, and B to page 139. They follow the instructions for negotiating an agreement between a car manufacturer and a distributor. Give students time to work out what they want to achieve from the negotiations and how they are going to achieve it. Remind them of the *Key expressions*. You could give them a time limit to reach an agreement. Monitor, checking they are using the expressions correctly.

Exercise 7

After the negotiation has finished, ask each student to make notes on questions 1–4. Then ask students, in pairs or small groups, to compare notes.

Finally, ask students to report back on each of the questions for whole-class feedback.

Photocopiable worksheet

Download and photocopy *Unit 11 Business communication worksheet* from the teacher resources in the *Online practice*.

Talking point

Tell students they are going to play a game where they have to negotiate in order to make progress. Allow students time to read the instructions and start the activity. For each situation they will be given two options, a or b. They will be sent to different situations depending on what they choose. Make sure the students are taking time to discuss each option carefully, before moving to the next box. This should generate a number of first and second conditionals. You could give them a time limit for each discussion and perhaps a signal to move on, to keep the game moving smoothly.

Do the first situation with the whole class to model the activity if you think it is necessary.

You could help students by checking some of the vocabulary before they start, for example, *panic, patriotic, rival, compromise, scapegoat, leak*. Monitor for correct use of conditional forms throughout the game.

ONE-TO-ONE Play the game with the student. At each stage, ask him/her to read the information and make a decision about what to do next. Before moving to the next stage, he/she should explain and justify his/her decision to you.

Progress test

Download and photocopy *Unit 11 Progress test* and *Speaking test* from the teacher resources in the *Online practice*.

12 Innovation

Unit content

By the end of this unit, students will be able to

- talk about innovative ideas
- talk about extremes
- praise and thank people formally and informally
- present new ideas.

Context

The topic of *Innovation* gives students the language to describe innovation and originality. It is essential for companies to innovate, reinvent and develop a successful approach to modernization in order to survive in the global business world. To do this, learners cover the language needed to describe innovation, the challenge of change and reinvention, and overcome obstacles in a world dominated by technology.

It is important to recognize the work of innovators and to celebrate new ideas. To do this, students will practise superlative forms and their use with structures such as the present perfect, and compare and rank achievements. Students will learn how to praise and thank people in a work environment. They also work on formal and informal expressions, and learn where to use the appropriate forms.

In this unit, students will also work on how to present new ideas using visuals. They learn how to structure presentations and use expressions to signpost that structure. They will also give a short presentation using a visual and assess how well the presentation followed the structure.

In the *Talking point*, students will have the opportunity to examine the effect that sound and music have in the retail sector. They will read about research on the effects of music on shopping habits and how different music or sounds have a noticeable effect on sales. They will then decide on the associations different musical genres have and recommend a particular genre for a particular business situation. Finally, they will present their ideas to the class and compare suggestions.

Starting point

Students work in pairs to answer the first question. Ask students to compare their responses with their partner's. They could then compare their answers in small groups, and then the group states which was the most popular time and place. The second question can be done with the whole class or in pairs before whole-class feedback. Encourage students to develop their answers.

PRE-WORK LEARNERS Ask students when and where they get their best ideas – in the middle of the night, while relaxing, while exercising, in the shower, when they are alone, when they are with other people?

Working with words

Exercise 1

Allow students a few minutes to think about the questions and then ask them to discuss their ideas with a partner.

> **Possible answers**
> It's important to help businesses stay competitive, keep their customers and attract new customers. Older companies could invest in training in new technologies and trends in their industries. They could have a policy of making sure a certain percentage of their workforce is young and newly qualified to help them become aware of new trends, both in the industry and in customer behaviours.

Exercise 2

Ask students to look at the picture and decide what is happening. Ask them if they have heard of Cirque du Soleil, and if they have, what they think of it. Ask students to look at the headings and then read the article. Tell students it's not necessary to understand all the words at this stage, only the general sense. They can then discuss the answers with a partner. Provide feedback on answers with the whole class.

> **Answers**
> Paragraph 1 b
> Paragraph 2 c
> Paragraph 3 a

Exercise 3

Ask students to work in pairs and answer the questions. Provide whole-class feedback by asking two or three students to report back on the answers.

> **Possible answers**
> The main challenge for Cirque du Soleil is to live up to the audience's expectations and create something new each season to keep audiences coming back for more.
> Their solution is to innovate and reinvent, perhaps to look for new performers to bring something different or more daring to the Cirque.
> The same is probably true for any type of business in order to survive. They have to keep their customers' expectations and changing needs in mind when developing products and services.

Exercise 4

Ask students to read the article in **2** again quickly and match the definitions 1–9 to the words in bold highlighted in the article. Let students compare answers with a partner. Check answers in whole-class feedback.

Answers
1 concept
2 brainchild
3 innovative
4 reinvention
5 revolutionize
6 catalyst
7 come up with
8 obstacle
9 original

EXTENSION Ask students to write nine sentences, one for each of the words. Then ask them to work in pairs. They take turns to read out their sentences to another pair, without the word from **4**, and the second pair has to guess which word is missing in the sentence. Monitor, checking they are using the words correctly.

Exercise 5

▶ **12.1** Tell students they are going to listen to three conversations about change or innovation. Tell them to match conversations 1–3 to the topics a–c. Play the listening. Let students check their answers with a partner. Then provide whole-class feedback and, if necessary, play the listening again, pausing to elicit the answers.

Answers
a 2   b 3   c 1

Exercise 6

▶ **12.1** Tell students to look at the list of adjectives and match them to conversations 1–3. They can check their answers with a partner. Play the listening again and tell students to check their answers. Check answers in whole-class feedback. If necessary, play the listening again, pausing for students to write down the adjectives.

Answers
1 traditional, reliable, dynamic, up-to-date
2 revolutionary, sophisticated
3 simple, original

PRONUNCIATION Draw the stress patterns for the words in **6** on the board. Ask students to work in pairs and say the words. They decide which stress pattern fits each word. Check the answers in open class and then ask students to spend a few minutes practising the words.

Answers

Oo	oOo	ooO	oOoo	oOooo	ooOoo
simple	dynamic	up-to-date	reliable traditional original	sophisticated	revolutionary

Further practice

If students need more practice, go to *Practice file 12* on page 128 of the *Student's Book*.

Exercise 7

Students work in pairs. Ask them to discuss the two questions. They could then join with another pair and compare their answers.

PRE-WORK LEARNERS Students could talk about their college or university for question 1, or they could talk about the job they would like to have. For question 2, they can concentrate on technology at home.

Exercise 8

Students work in small groups. Tell them to read the quotes from people talking about ideas and obstacles in their lives. Refer students to the *Tip* and ask them to give an example of an *innovation* and an example of an *invention*. Give them a few minutes to think about different ways they could help the people. Then ask students to discuss their suggestions and come to a group decision on the best ways to help. They can then tell the whole class what their suggestions are.

Possible answers
1 Is there a family member who can look after the children? If you get together with several other people who also have pre-school children, then you could take turns to look after all the children.
2 Have you tried crowdfunding? What about talking to motorcycle shops/manufacturers in your area?
3 You could do some volunteering in local charities. You could look for crowdfunding schemes. You could work freelance.

ONE-TO-ONE Ask the student to think about two or three different ways to help each person. He/she tells you the ways he/she has thought of. Discuss them with the student with reference to the questions in **9**.

Exercise 9

Students work in pairs. Try to make sure the two students worked in different groups in **8**. Tell them to report their group discussion to each other and answer the questions. You could ask them to present the best 'brainchild' and how they overcame any obstacles they met, to the whole class.

Photocopiable worksheet

Download and photocopy *Unit 12 Working with words worksheet* from the teacher resources in the *Online practice*.

Language at work

Exercise 1

Ask students to look at the picture on the left and decide what is happening. Ask them to look at the title of the press release, read the article and answer the questions with a partner. Ask one or two pairs to give feedback to the whole class.

Possible answers
These events can be important for publicity and advertising. Winning an award can make people think of a company in a very positive way. It also helps all the companies in an industry to be aware of developments and innovations.

Exercise 2

Tell students to read the press release again and answer the questions. Let them compare answers with a partner. Check the answers in whole-class feedback.

Answers
1 No, it's 'one' of a few events.
2 In 2001.
3 The best new inventors and innovators that year.
4 The second and third highest achievers receive a platinum or silver award.

Exercise 3

Ask students to read the press release in **1** again and underline the superlative adjectives. Then ask them to decide which are regular and which are irregular. Let students check their answers with a partner and then do whole-class feedback.

Answers

Underline: the most important, the earliest, the best, third and second highest
Regular forms: (one of) the most important, the earliest, (third and second) highest
Irregular: the best

Exercise 4

Refer sudents to the *Language point*. Tell students to read extracts a–d and match them to explanations 1–4. Students compare answers with a partner and then do whole-class feedback.

Answers

1 d **2** b **3** a **4** c

Grammar reference

If students need more information, go to *Grammar reference* on page 129 of the *Student's Book*.

Exercise 5

Students work in pairs. Ask them to read the sentences and say the same thing in a different way, using a superlative form.

Answers

1 This is one of the most important conferences this month.
2 These are the highest profits (that) I've ever seen.
3 The XP55 is now our second highest-selling product.
4 In the last century, I think the microchip has had the biggest impact of any invention.

EXTRA ACTIVITY

Students work in pairs or small groups. Write some adjectives on the board, for example, *long, high, expensive, cold, large, heavy, spoken, near, successful, (good)-selling,* and ask students to make them superlatives. Then divide the class into two groups, A and B. Give each group five prompts and ask them to make questions for a general knowledge quiz. You could ask them to give options with the questions. They can check the answers on the Internet. For example:

Group A:

1 2nd longest river / world: Which is the second longest river in the world?
   a) the Amazon b) the Danube c) the Mississippi
The Amazon, although some think the Amazon is longer than the Nile, traditionally thought to be the longest; it depends on how they are measured.

2 most expensive painting ever sold: Which is the most expensive painting ever sold?
   a) Van Gogh's *Sunflowers* b) Picasso's *Les Femmes d'Alger* c) Rembrandt's *Self portrait*
In 2015 it was Picasso's *Les Femmes d'Alger*, sold for $179 million, the highest price ever paid for a painting.

3 coldest place / Earth: Which is the coldest place on Earth?
   a) Siberia b) the Arctic c) the Antarctic
The current record low of minus 89.2°C was measured in Antarctica, at the Russian Vostok base, on 21 July 1983.

4 planet nearest / sun: Which is the nearest planet to the sun?
   a) Venus b) Mars c) Mercury
Mercury is the nearest planet to the sun.

5 best-selling album / all time: Which is the best-selling album of all time?
   a) The Beatles *Greatest Hits* b) Michael Jackson *Thriller* c) Adele *21*
Thriller by Michael Jackson is recorded as the best-selling album up to 2015.

Group B:

1 highest mountain / Africa: Which is the highest mountain in Africa?
   a) Mount Kilimanjaro b) Mount Kenya c) The Drakensberg
Mount Kilimanjaro is the highest mountain in Africa.

2 most successful film / 21st century: What's the most successful film of the 21st century?
   a) Titanic b) Batman vs Superman c) Avatar
In 2015, Avatar is the most successful film of the 21st century.

3 largest ocean / world: Which is the largest ocean in the world?
   a) the Pacific b) the Atlantic C) the Indian
The Pacific is the largest ocean in the world.

4 most spoken language / world: Which is the most spoken language in the world?
   a) English b) Hindi c) Chinese
Chinese is the most spoken language in the world.

5 oldest university / the world: Where is the oldest university in the world?
   a) Fez, Morocco b) Oxford, England c) Bologna, Italy
The oldest university in the world is the University of Karueein, founded in 859 CE in Fez, Morocco.

Further practice

If students need more practice, go to *Practice file 12* on page 129 of the *Student's Book*.

Exercise 6

Students make sentences about their business using the phrases. Then they take turns to tell a partner their sentences and explain their answers. Monitor, checking students are using the correct superlative forms.

PRE-WORK LEARNERS Ask students to make sentences about their college using these phrases:

1 … is one of the most popular subjects to study.
2 … is the most difficult subject to do well in.
3 … is the most popular sport.

4 … is the department with the most undergraduate students.

5 … is the department with the least hard-working students.

Then they take turns with a partner to tell them their sentences and explain their answers. Monitor, checking students are using the correct superlative forms.

Exercise 7

Students work in pairs. Give them time to think of the questions and answers and the correct adjective forms to use. They can then take turns asking the questions and comparing answers. Monitor, checking they are using the correct superlative forms.

Photocopiable worksheet

Download and photocopy *Unit 12 Language at work worksheet* from the teacher resources in the *Online practice*.

Practically speaking

Exercise 1

Ask students to discuss the questions with a partner. Make sure they understand *praise* here, i.e. to acknowledge someone has worked hard or done a particularly good job. Tell them that they can use their own personal experience to explain their answers.

Exercise 2

▶ **12.2** Tell students they are going to listen and match conversations 1–3 to situations a–c. Play the listening. Let them check their answers with a partner. Check the answers in whole-class feedback. If necessary, play the listening again, pausing to elicit the correct answers.

> **Answers**
> a 2   b 1   c 3

Exercise 3

▶ **12.2** Tell students to read the expressions and then listen again to the conversations. Play the listening again. Ask students to work in pairs and decide if the expressions are normally formal (F) or informal (I). These ideas of formal and informal are guidelines rather than absolutes. Some of the informal expressions, especially 2 and 5, may be heard in more formal situations. Also, formal expressions such as 1, 4 and 7, can be heard in less formal situations.

> **Suggested answers**
> 1 F   2 I   3 F   4 F   5 I   6 F   7 F   8 I   9 F   10 I

Exercise 4

Ask students to write down three jobs they have completed recently. Then, working in pairs, they take turns to tell each other about what they have done. They should try to vary the situations, having some formal and some informal. Provide whole-class feedback by asking two or three pairs to report what they said for each situation, and why they decided it was formal or informal.

PRE-WORK LEARNERS Ask students to think about their projects and assignments, particularly if there's something that they did in a group. They then take turns to tell each other about them, and then praise and/or thank each other.

Business communication

Exercise 1

Ask students to read the mission statement and discuss the questions with a partner. Check answers in whole-class feedback by asking two or three students to report back.

PRE-WORK LEARNERS Ask students to think about their school or college. Does it have a set of principles or ideals? What are they? Where do they expect to find them?

In small groups, ask students to write the ideal mission statement/principles of a college or university.

Exercise 2

▶ **12.3** Explain to students that they are going to listen to part of a meeting at Bertran RL. The meeting is to discuss the company's mission statement in **1**. Ask students to read the question and the aims to know what to listen for. Play the listening. Let students check their answers with a partner. Check answers with the whole class.

> **Answers**
> B and C

Exercise 3

▶ **12.3** Students work in pairs. Before they listen, ask them to read the expressions from the team leader's presentation and put them in the correct order 1–8 (1 and 8 have already been completed). Then play the listening again to check the answers. If necessary, pause it and elicit the correct answers.

> **Answers**
> 4 First, I'm going to talk …
> 1 Good morning, everyone, and thanks for coming.
> 2 We have a lot to do, so let's start.
> 8 Feel free to ask questions …
> 3 I'd like to begin by explaining …
> 6 The main reason for this meeting is to …
> 7 so finally we'll …
> 5 Then, we'll try to …

Exercise 4

▶ **12.4** Tell students to look at the slide before they listen. Ask them to answer the question while they listen. Let students compare their answers with a partner. Check answers in whole-class feedback.

> **Answers**
> The words on the slide represent the answers given by old and new customers to the question 'What words describe Bertran RL?'

Exercise 5

▶ **12.4** Students work in pairs. Ask them to try to fill in the gaps before they listen. Then play the listening again for them to check their answers. Check answers in whole-class feedback.

> **Answers**
> 1 look at
> 2 can see
> 3 You'll notice that

Exercise 6

▶ **12.5** Tell students they are going to listen to the final part of the team leader's presentation. Ask students to listen for the expressions he uses to signal the end of the presentation and to check if everyone has understood. You could ask students to write down the expressions. Let students compare their answers with a partner. Check answers in whole-class feedback.

> **Answers**
> That's everything I want to say for the moment.
> Thank you all for listening.
> Are there any questions?

Further practice
If students need more practice, go to *Practice file 12* on page 128 of the *Student's Book*.

Exercise 7
Explain to students that they are going to work individually to give a two-minute presentation. First of all, though, they have to design a slide with adjectives they think or hope their customers use, similar to the slide in **4**. Remind students that 'less is more' with slides and that they should not put too many words, too many colours, or too many different fonts on the slide. Refer students to the *Key expressions* to help them express their ideas and structure the presentation.

If it is not possible to use slides in class, then students can write on large pieces of paper instead.

PRE-WORK LEARNERS Tell students to give a two-minute presentation on one of these topics.

- buying a smartphone
- opening a bank account
- buying exercise equipment

They should design a slide with adjectives that they associate with the product or service, similar to the slide in **4**.

Exercise 8
Put students in small groups to give their presentations. They take turns to present their slide, remembering to introduce themselves and the presentation. They give reasons for each adjective, then they end the presentation and invite questions. Those listening to the presentations could think of at least one question to ask the presenter.

Finally, ask each group to report back and say what made the most successful presentations.

ALTERNATIVE You could ask students in each group to give feedback on the presentations. You could give them a tick list, for example:

Introduced him/herself	Y/N
Introduced the slide using the phrases	Y/N
Explained the visual using the phrases	Y/N
Finished off using the phrases	Y/N
Thanked everyone for listening	Y/N
Invited questions	Y/N

Photocopiable worksheet
Download and photocopy *Unit 12 Business communication worksheet* from the teacher resources in the *Online practice*.

Talking point

Discussion

Exercise 1
Ask students to read the article and answer the question, reminding them to give reasons. Ask two or three students for their ideas for feedback.

Exercise 2
Ask students to discuss the background music and their reaction to it with a partner. Check answers by asking one or two pairs for their ideas.

Exercise 3
Ask students to discuss the questions with a partner. Check answers by asking one or two pairs for feedback.

Task

Exercise 1
▶ **12.6** Put students in small groups and tell them to listen to the six different types of music and match them to the words. Check the answers in whole-class feedback.

> **Answers**
> | | | | |
> |---|---|---|---|
> | 1 | classical | 4 | opera |
> | 2 | pop | 5 | Bollywood |
> | 3 | rock | 6 | jazz |

Exercise 2
▶ **12.6** Still in their groups, ask students to come up with products or services they might associate with each of the types of music. Play the listening again. Students may want to hear some extracts a couple of times to make their decisions.

> **Possible answers**
> Classical – beautiful interiors, the countryside, expensive cars
> Pop – children's toys, sweets, teens – clothes, make-up, entertainment
> Rock – cars, motorcycles, clothes, mobile phones
> Opera – city break in Vienna, Milan, etc., comic takes on services (insurance comparison companies in UK)
> Bollywood – exotic holidays abroad, restaurants
> Jazz – something very cool, perhaps clothes, something American or French

Exercise 3
In their groups, students discuss the situations and decide what type of music or sounds they would recommend. They should give good business reasons for their choices. Tell them they are going to present their choices to the whole class. Make sure they introduce themselves, explain each idea clearly, finish the presentation and invite questions. If necessary, remind them of the *Key expressions* on page 82.

ONE-TO-ONE Let the student choose one of the situations and present his/her ideas.

Exercise 4
Each group presents their ideas to the class. Those listening to the presentations should ask questions at the end. The class can then decide which ideas worked best for each situation.

Progress test
Download and photocopy *Unit 12 Progress test* and *Speaking test* from the teacher resources in the *Online practice*.

Preview

The topic of this *Viewpoint* is *The Falkirk Wheel*. In this *Viewpoint*, students begin by watching and discussing a video of five people talking about transport problems in their city and how they have found solutions to them. Students then watch and discuss two more videos: one about the history of canals in the UK and another about the Falkirk Wheel – an ingenious piece of engineering that has solved the problem of height differences between the Forth and Clyde canal, and the Union canal, in Scotland. Finally, students do a task which involves giving a tour of the Falkirk Wheel.

Exercise 1

▶ **01** Before students watch the video, ask them to list the most common methods of transport used in their city or country. Ask students to read the questions and make notes while they are watching. Play the video and, if necessary, pause after each speaker to allow writing time. Check answers as a whole class.

Answers

	What kind of transport problems does their city have?	What is their solution?
Speaker 1	Milan: not suited to cars	introduced traffic controlled zone
Speaker 2	Brussels: infrequent metro or bus service; public transport system doesn't cover all places; traffic jams especially at rush hour; aggressive drivers; dangerous to cycle	try to cycle; try to use public transport; use car-sharing scheme
Speaker 3	Oxford: not built for cars, buses, lorries	travel by train; stay on boat and commute on foot
Speaker 4	Oxford: bad traffic problems; don't live on a bus route	use a motorcycle; quicker to walk or cycle
Speaker 5	Oxford: traffic congestion; most people commute into the city	lives on a canal boat so can live closer to city centre and cycle to work

Exercise 2

Ask students to discuss the transport problems in their city or country with a partner, and explain their own solutions. You could check answers with one or two pairs in whole-class feedback.

ONE-TO-ONE Ask the student about transport problems in his/her city and how he/she overcomes them. Ask him/her how transport has changed in the past 50 years, and if there are any plans for changes in the near future.

Exercise 3

Ask students to look at the picture of the canal and answer the questions. The boat in the picture, which is called a *narrowboat* (but is sometimes referred to as a *barge*), is passing through a lock. These narrowboats were traditionally used to transport cargo, but are now more commonly used as accommodation, often for holidays.

Exercise 4

Ask students to read the definitions a–g and match them to the words 1–7. Check they understand what is meant by the *Industrial Revolution*: The Industrial Revolution was the transition from a mainly agricultural and rural society to one which was based on manufacturing, and became mainly urban. It occurred between the 1760s and the 1830s. Make sure students notice the distinction between *loch* and *lock*. *Loch* comes from the Scottish Gaelic word for *lake*, and is pronounced with a guttural *ch* ending: /lɒx/. However, the words *lock* (on a canal) and *loch* are sometimes pronounced in the same way in England: /lɒk/. This is because the guttural *ch* sound is not standard in English. Check answers in whole-class feedback.

Answers
1 c 2 a 3 d 4 b 5 g 6 f 7 e

Exercise 5

▶ **02** Ask students to read the list of scenes A–G and tell them to number the scenes in the order they first see them as they watch the video. You could turn the sound off and do this exercise with no narration to help students focus only on the images. They could also predict what they think the narrator will say using the words from **4**. Play the video. Let students check their answers with a partner. Check answers with the whole class. Note that there may be some variation, as some elements appear more than once (e.g. locks on a canal).

Answers
A 5 B 6 C 1 D 4 E 3 F 7 G 2

VIDEO SCRIPT

Today, we transport goods across countries and around the world without thinking. Ships arrive at international ports and road and railway networks carry the products we use every day to their destination. We can't imagine life before this. How did business and industry function before the invention of the internal combustion engine and the railways?

In the United Kingdom as well as in many other countries, water has always been important in the country's transportation. During the British Industrial Revolution in the eighteenth and early nineteenth centuries, heavy goods were carried up and down Britain's canals. By the mid-nineteenth century, Britain had connected the country with a network of canals and rivers. Seven thousand kilometres of waterways linked the new industrial cities across the United Kingdom. The construction of these canals was one of greatest innovations of the Industrial Revolution.

But the use of canals didn't last long for two reasons. One problem was that the United Kingdom isn't flat. Its hills and mountains were an enormous challenge for engineers. This presented a huge obstacle for the canal builders. They had to build locks so boats could go up and down. This made transportation by canal very slow. Instead, with the arrival of the steam train, a system of railways was quickly built and so the canals were used less and less until many were closed.

In more recent years however, some canals have been restored and reopened. Now they are used for a very different kind of business. The tourism and leisure industry rents canal boats, and many people spend long weekends or holidays cruising through the countryside on a houseboat.

Exercise 6

▶ 02 Ask students to read the questions carefully and check what they are listening for. Play the video again. Let students check their answers with a partner. Check answers in whole-class feedback. If necessary, pause after the relevant part of the video for students to hear the words and phrases for the answers.

Answers
1 Because of the Industrial Revolution and the need to transport heavy goods
2 7,000 kilometres
3 The construction of the canals
4 The hills and mountains
5 The steam train
6 The tourism and leisure industry

Exercise 7

Ask students to discuss the questions in small groups. Ask one or two groups to report their discussion to the whole class as feedback.

Possible answer
Students can refer to building regeneration programmes in their own cities, or examples of brownfield sites (previously used and now disused industrial/commercial sites) being turned into modern housing. Alternatively, modern apps like Uber and Airbnb are good examples of taking an old business idea (e.g. taxis and accommodation) and reusing it in a new way.

Exercise 8

▶ 03 Give students time to read the questions and options. Play the video. Ask students to choose the correct options and check their choices with a partner. Check answers in whole-class feedback.

Answers
1 c 2 a 3 b

VIDEO SCRIPT

In Scotland, the Forth and Clyde and Union canals connect the cities of Edinburgh and Glasgow. They pass through some of Scotland's beautiful lochs and mountains. When they were first built, the canals had a series of eleven locks near the town of Falkirk, which allowed the boats to go up and down a height of 35 metres. But in 1933 the locks were closed down and so no boats could make the journey between the two cities anymore.

Then, in 1994, a team of engineers used modern technology to open the canal at Falkirk again and, after years of research and development, engineers came up with an innovative solution to the challenge. The Falkirk Wheel is 35 metres tall. It was built with 1,200 tonnes of steel and cost over £17 million to build. It opened to the public in 2002 and is a popular tourist attraction.

The basic concept behind the Falkirk Wheel is quite simple. Two boats can enter at each end of the wheel. The weight of the water

and the boat at each end is always equal. Because the weight is balanced perfectly, not much energy is needed to turn the wheel. In fact, it lifts boats up and down in four minutes using less power than it takes to boil eight kettles.

Two hundred years after the first canals were built, the Falkirk Wheel is a classic example of how original thinking and up-to-date technology can breathe new life into the old ways of doing things. And who knows? As we look for alternative types of energy in the future, maybe one day we'll return to the canals for more of our transportation needs.

Exercise 9

▶ 03 Ask students to look at the numbers and years. You could ask them to discuss with a partner what they can remember about these from the video. Because this task requires intensive listening, you could turn the screen off so students only listen this time round, which might help their note-taking. Play the video/listening. Let students check their answers with a partner. Check answers in whole-class feedback. Play the video again if necessary, pausing at the numbers for students to hear the answers.

Answers
2 This is the year when the locks were closed down so no boats could travel between Edinburgh and Glasgow.
3 This is the year when engineers started working on the Falkirk Wheel.
4 The Falkirk Wheel is 35 metres tall.
5 1,200 tonnes of steel was used to build the Falkirk Wheel.
6 This is the cost to build the Falkirk Wheel.
7 This is when the Falkirk Wheel opened to the public.
8 Two boats can enter at each end of the Falkirk Wheel at the same time.
9 It takes four minutes to lift boats up and down.

Exercise 10

Explain to students that they are going to give the commentary to the video with the sound off. They work in two groups, A and B. Ask them to read the instructions for either Student A or Student B and prepare what they are going to say. Then put students into AB pairs and ask them to do the tour.

When the students are doing this, it might be helpful to pause the video at certain stages to give students more time to develop their conversation; then, when you feel students have run out of something to say, you continue playing the video.

Exercise 11

Students can then swap roles and repeat the exercise in **10**.

ONE-TO-ONE Ask the student to prepare the tour as a guide and present it to you. Tell him/her you will be asking questions. If the Internet is available, you could ask him/her to look up the Falkirk Wheel online to get more information for the tour.

Further video ideas
You can find a list of suggested ideas for how to use video in the class in the teacher resources in the *Online practice*.

Unit content

By the end of this unit, students will be able to
- talk about breakdowns and faults
- use relative pronouns
- check someone understands
- discuss and solve problems.

Context

The topic of *Breakdowns* gives students the language to describe problems, breakdowns and faults, and find solutions. These occur in all sectors of business and it is essential they are spotted, diagnosed and resolved in the most efficient and effective way. To do this, students cover the language needed to describe problems in many areas, such as software, retail and communications.

It is important to be able to define the problem and solution, clearly and accurately. To help students do this, they will learn about using defining relative clauses. They will also practise defining people, objects, places and times.

In this unit, students will also work on how to check that someone understands. It is very important when giving instructions or solving a problem that the instructions are clear and that everyone understands. Students will discuss various topics and problems, giving a detailed description of the situation, then give their ideas and check the listener understands.

In the *Talking point*, students have the opportunity to assess the importance of public relations to a business. They will read about a public relations disaster and the effect it had on a multinational company. They will then discuss various situations and how public relations can be used to help deal with the problem. Finally, they will present their ideas to the class and compare suggestions.

Starting point

Do the first question with the whole class. Ask them how they feel about companies that produce goods and provide services that are not 100% perfect. The second question can be done with the whole class or in pairs before whole-class feedback. Encourage students to develop their answers, giving reasons why they would or wouldn't buy these goods.

Working with words

Exercise 1

Allow students a few minutes to think about the questions and then ask them to discuss their ideas with a partner. Provide whole-class feedback by asking two or three pairs to describe their breakdowns. You could find out which are the most prevalent.

Possible answers
Transport: cars breaking down or having faults / train or bus services that are consistently late, or flight delays or cancellations due to weather or industrial action
Work: computers crashing, heating or air conditioning failures, orders not arriving / not being dispatched on time
Communications: misunderstandings, pressing 'Reply all' when sending a sensitive email

PRE-WORK LEARNERS Ask students to think of times that there have been breakdowns at their college, for example, confusion about rooms to go to, timetable errors, important messages not going to the right person, etc. Ask them to discuss what happened and how the problem was resolved.

Exercise 2

Ask students to look at the headings, read the news stories and complete the table. Tell students it's not necessary to understand all the words at this stage, only the general sense. They can then discuss the answers with a partner. Provide feedback on answers with the whole class.

Answers

What type of breakdown or fault?	Who did it affect?	Have they solved the problem?
1 Software / IT	Doctors, nurses (and patients)	Yes. Late last night.
2 Defect in car gearbox	Car owners	No. Car owners must take the car into garages to fix it.
3 Metal bits in macaroni and cheese boxes	Shoppers and the manufacturer	No, not yet.
4 Misunderstandings in internal communications	Staff at an Australian company	Yes. Staff have to use instant messaging.

Exercise 3

Ask students to read the news stories in **2** again, find the pairs of words and match each to its correct definition, a or b. Let students compare answers with a partner. Check answers in whole-class feedback.

> **Answers**
> 1 a failure b go down
> 2 a fault b defect
> 3 a damage b injury
> 4 a resolve b complaint
> 5 a refund b recall
> 6 a misunderstanding b mistake

EXTENSION You could ask students to write a sentence for each pair of words. They take turns to read the sentence without saying the word. Their partner then says which of the words it is. Monitor, checking they are using the words accurately.

Exercise 4

Students work in small groups to discuss the problems. Remind them to use the words from **3**, changing the form where necessary. Monitor, checking they are using the correct form of the words. Provide whole-class feedback by asking a different group to give feedback on each situation. The class could then compare their ideas.

Exercise 5

Tell students to read the two sentences from the first news story in **2** and answer the questions. Let them check their answers with a partner. Then provide whole-class feedback, eliciting why the answers are correct.

> **Answers**
> 1 *Caused* is a verb, simple past form, and *as a result of* is a connector, connecting the first sentence to the second by giving the result of the event in the first sentence.
> 2 *A software problem* is the cause and *all the computers to go down for 24 hours yesterday* is the result.
> 3 *The system failure* is the cause, and refers back to the event described in the first sentence, and *doctors and nurses couldn't access patients' medical records* is the result.
> 4 Text 2: *because of* (cause), *lead to* (result), *doesn't cause* (result)
> Text 3: *resulted in* (result)
> Text 4: *due to* (cause), *because* (cause)

Exercise 6

Tell students to work in pairs. Students match causes 1–4 to results a–d. Check answers in whole-class feedback.

> **Possible answers**
> 2 a No training with the new cutting equipment resulted in an injury to an employee's hand.
> 3 d As a result of new software, there was a systems failure with the database.
> 4 b Poor language skills led to misunderstandings between office branches.

Further practice

If students need more practice, go to *Practice file 13* on page 130 of the *Student's Book*.

Exercise 7

Tell students to discuss three recent breakdowns, faults or problems at work with a partner. Ask them to give details of the causes and results of these problems. You could ask them what solution the company came up with.

> **Possible answers**
> Company server goes down, causing problems communicating with distributors and customers.
> The heating breaks down in winter, and the offices become very cold. People start catching colds and staying off work.
> An important delivery does not arrive for one of your most important customers and you are having great difficulty tracking it.
> Your company has decided to refurbish the offices and the decorators are behind schedule.
> The fire inspection team has decided that the fire escape measures are inadequate and they want the company to improve the fire precautions and escape routes.

PRE-WORK LEARNERS Students could talk about recent problems in their college or university. If they need encouragement, then suggest things like a misunderstanding between classmates, an accident in the college or while travelling to college, problems travelling to college – car breakdown / bicycle puncture or broken chain / bus strike, something they recently bought that developed a fault or had a defect, etc. Monitor, checking they are using the verbs and connectors to express cause and result correctly.

Photocopiable worksheet

Download and photocopy *Unit 13 Working with words worksheet* from the teacher resources in the *Online practice*.

Language at work

Exercise 1

Ask students to look at the pictures and say what they can see and what they think the connection between them is. Ask one or two students to give feedback to the whole class. Don't give the students all the information at this time as they will find it out in the following exercises.

Exercise 2

▶ **13.1** Tell students to listen to part of a radio programme and answer the question. Play the listening. Let them compare answers with a partner. Check the answers in whole-class feedback.

> **Answers**
> Post-it notes and Alexander Fleming discovering penicillin.

Exercise 3

▶ **13.1** Ask students to read the sentences and complete them with a relative pronoun from the list. Let them check their answers with a partner, then play the listening again so students can check their answers. Do whole-class feedback. If necessary, play the listening again, pausing it to elicit the correct answers.

Answers
1 which
2 who
3 that
4 whose
5 when
6 where

Exercise 4

Tell students to complete the *Language point* by matching the relative pronouns in **3** to the explanations. Students compare answers with a partner and then do whole-class feedback.

Answers
which, who, whose, when, where

Grammar reference

If students need more information, go to *Grammar reference* on page 131 of the *Student's Book*.

Exercise 5

Students work in pairs. Ask them to read each group of sentences. Refer them to the *Tip*. They then join the sentences using one of the relative pronouns from the list. Provide whole-class feedback, eliciting why each answer is correct.

Answers
1 It was accidentally discovered by an engineer who worked for Canon. One day, his pen fired ink out when he rested a hot iron on it by accident.
2 The Carey Moon Lake House was a restaurant where George Crum worked as a chef. One day, Crum had a complaining customer whose potatoes were 'too soft and thick'. In the end, Crum made extremely thin, hard potatoes that eventually became famous as 'crisps'.

Exercise 6

Students complete the sentences about themselves and their work so they are true for them, using relative pronouns. Then they take turns with a partner to tell them their sentences and explain their answers. Monitor, checking students are using the relative pronouns correctly.

PRE-WORK LEARNERS Ask students to think about their college and make sentences that are true for them using these prompts:

1 A useful subject to study is one …
2 A good teacher is someone …
3 My busiest time of day is …
4 We're a college whose students are …
5 Our main building is a place …

ONE-TO-ONE Ask the student to complete the sentences so they are true for him/her and then ask him/her to give examples and reasons for his/her statements.

Further practice

If students need more practice, go to *Practice file 13* on page 131 of the *Student's Book*.

Exercise 7

Ask students to work in pairs. Give them time to think of at least one object, one person, one place or one time. The students take turns to define each without saying the word, and their partner has to try to work out what it is. Monitor, checking they are using the correct relative pronouns.

Photocopiable worksheet

Download and photocopy *Unit 13 Language at work worksheet* from the teacher resources in the *Online practice*.

Practically speaking

Exercise 1

▶ **13.2** Tell students they are going to listen to four conversations about problems or difficulties. Ask them to listen and match the conversations 1–4 with the problems A–D. Play the listening. Let students compare their answers with a partner. Provide whole-class feedback. If necessary, play the listening again, pausing to elicit the correct answers.

Answers
A 3 **B** 1 **C** 4 **D** 2

Exercise 2

▶ **13.2** Students work in pairs. Ask them to match the question stems 1–4 to a–d to form complete questions. Play the listening again. Check the answers in whole-class feedback. If necessary, play the listening again, pausing to elicit the correct answers.

Answers
1 d 2 a 3 b 4 c

Exercise 3

▶ **13.2** Tell students to listen again and decide if the listener understands what the first person is saying in each conversation. Play the listening again. Check answers in whole-class feedback.

Answers
1 Yes
2 No
3 No
4 Yes

Exercise 4

Ask students to work in pairs and to look at the responses. They decide which ones show the listener understands, doesn't understand or partially understands. Check answers in whole-class feedback.

Answers
1 U 2 PU 3 DU 4 U

PRONUNCIATION To focus on the pronunciation of fixed phrases, ask students to look at the phrases in **2** and decide how to link them and where to put the stress/intonation. Then listen to **13.2** again to check.

*Do you **know** what I **mean**?* /dəjə`neʊwɒtaɪ`miːn/
*Does that **make sense**?* /dʌzðæ(t)meɪk`sens/
*Is that **clear**?* / əzðæɪzðæ(t)`klɪə(r)/
*Do you **see**?* /djə`siː/

Ask students to match a response in **4**, and to work out how to say it to sound sure, and to sound a bit hesitant when they don't or partially understand.

*Abso**lute**ly.* /ˌæbsəˈluːtli/

Kind *of, but…* /ˈkaɪndə bət/

*I **don't** get…* /aɪ ˈdəʊn(t) get/

*I see what you **mean**…* /aɪ siː wɒt juˈmiːn/

Then ask students to take turns checking and responding. Monitor, checking their linking and intonation.

Exercise 5

Students work in pairs. Give them time to prepare their explanations for the four prompts. Ask them to take turns to explain each one to their partner, and check they understand. The partner responds and asks for clarification when they don't, or only partially, understand. Monitor, checking that students are explaining clearly and responding with the appropriate expressions.

EXTENSION Ask students to take turns explaining one quite simple and two more complicated things to a partner. They should use the checking phrases and the responses to show when they understand, partially understand or don't understand. They could describe things like changing a bicycle tyre, uploading a new programme onto a computer, a recipe, a mathematical or scientific problem, how to get to a place by car or on public transport, how to recognize an important customer/person they are meeting at the airport. Provide whole-class feedback by getting two or three pairs to perform their conversations to the class.

Business communication

Exercise 1

Ask students to think about the question. Check answers in whole-class feedback by asking two or three students to report back.

Exercise 2

▶ **13.3** Explain to students that they are going to listen to two conversations about problems. Tell them to make notes in the table about what the problem is, the diagnosis and the solution. Play the listening. Let the students check their answers with a partner. Check the answers in whole-class feedback. If necessary, play the listening again, pausing to elicit the correct answers.

Answers

Problem	Diagnosis	Solution
1 Not enough time to complete a report and her boss keeps giving extra work.	There's a communication problem with her boss.	Talk to her boss and request an extension to the deadline for the report.
2 The laptop keeps going wrong.	It's old and there's probably a problem with the battery.	Use the cable and buy a new battery.

Exercise 3

▶ **13.3** Students work in pairs. Before they listen, ask them to read the expressions from the two conversations. Then play the listening again for students to number the expressions in the order they hear them. Check the answers in whole-class feedback. If necessary, play the listening again, pausing to elicit the correct answers.

Answers
Conversation 1
1 What's the matter?
5 Have you tried talking to her?
3 What do you mean by 'extra work'?
8 That should sort it out temporarily.
2 My boss keeps on giving me extra work.
6 I'd ask to speak to her if I were you.
7 I think you should ask for an extension.
4 It looks like you've got a communication problem to me.

Conversation 2
1 How can I help?
8 That should fix it.
2 It keeps on going wrong all the time.
4 It's always crashing and it won't remember the time or date.
3 What's wrong with it exactly?
6 It sounds as though it could be a battery problem.
7 The best thing would be to buy a new battery.
5 When you say 'it's always crashing', do you mean it actually switches off?

Further practice

If students need more practice, go to *Practice file 13* on page 130 of the *Student's Book*.

Exercise 4

Students work in pairs. Ask them to look at the flow chart and problems 1 and 2. Give students time to think about what they can say about the problems. Refer them to the *Key expressions*.

Then ask them to take turns starting the conversations. Monitor, checking that they are expressing the problems accurately, asking for details, diagnosing the problem, giving advice and confirming a solution.

Provide whole-class feedback by asking two or three pairs to perform their conversations to the class. You could ask the class if they think the advice the speakers gave will help solve the problem.

Exercise 5

Students work in groups. Ask each student to choose a problem and prepare to speak for at least one minute on it. Give them a few minutes to prepare. As each person speaks, the others listen. At the end of the speech they ask for more details and try to offer a solution. The group as a whole can decide on the best solution. Then each group reports back to the whole class.

PRE-WORK LEARNERS Ask the students to choose one of these topics and then follow the instructions for **5**:

• A problem with a piece of technology they use in college.

• A breakdown in communications between the administration and students at college.

• An unreliable or untrustworthy classmate.

ONE-TO-ONE Ask the student to choose one of the topics and prepare a one-minute talk on it. When he/she has finished, ask for more details on the topic. Then together try to come up with a good solution to the situation.

Photocopiable worksheet
Download and photocopy *Unit 13 Business communication worksheet* from the teacher resources in the *Online practice*.

Talking point

Discussion

Exercise 1
Ask students if they have heard of the Deepwater Horizon disaster. You could give a few cues, for example, *It happened in the USA and Gulf of Mexico, It happened in 2010, It involved oil*. Then ask students to read the article and answer the questions.

Exercise 2
Ask students to discuss the question and their attitude to the quotation with a partner. Check answers by asking one or two pairs for their ideas.

Exercise 3
Ask students to discuss the questions with a partner. Check answers by asking one or two pairs for their ideas. Ask students what other examples of negative publicity they can think of.

PRE-WORK LEARNERS Ask students if they have ever heard of a well-known company receiving negative publicity: What happened? How did the company handle the event? Did they follow the PR advice in the article?

Task

Exercise 1
Students work in groups. Ask them to read the three different public relations situations and discuss how they would deal with each. Tell the groups that they will have to present the situation, their diagnosis of it, and offer a solution, to the whole class. Give students time to organize their presentation.

ONE-TO-ONE Ask the student to read the three situations, choose one and make notes on how he/she would deal with it. Tell the student he/she can use previous experience if it's relevant. The student then presents his/her advice for the situation.

Exercise 2
Each group presents their ideas to the class. Those listening should ask questions at the end to clarify, and ask for more details. The class can then decide which advice would work best in each situation.

ALTERNATIVE Divide the class into three groups, A, B, C, and ask each group to read one of the three different public relations situations. The groups discuss how they would deal with the situation, what steps they would take to deal with the problem itself and how they would organize the PR. Ask them to make some notes so they can report their ideas to another group.

Now ask the groups to reform, with one or two As, Bs and Cs, in each group. They can then present their situations. The others listen, ask for clarification and decide whether they think the advice will work.

These new groups, as a whole, decide on the best solutions for each of the problems.

Progress test
Download and photocopy *Unit 13 Progress test* and *Speaking test* from the teacher resources in the *Online practice*.

Unit content

By the end of this unit, students will be able to
- talk about, describe and explain processes
- use passive forms to describe processes
- explain a process in stages
- deal with questions after a presentation.

Context

The topic of *Processes* gives students the language to talk about, describe and explain processes. Anybody who works, or plans to work, in business knows that it is essential to be able to describe accurately what your company does, as well as how the different processes and systems work within the company. To do this, students cover the language needed to describe the stages of a process, and learn how to describe the process itself and present an action plan using common multi-word verbs.

To describe processes accurately and succinctly, it is essential to be able to use passive forms. To do this, students will practise using passive forms in different tenses and identify where to use passive and active forms. Students will also learn how to describe their own company's products and services.

In this unit, students will work on how to explain a process using expressions to signpost its stages. They will also learn how to deal with questions when giving a short presentation.

In the *Talking point*, students will read about 'Lean Coffee' meetings and the thinking and process behind these. They will then have the opportunity to hold a meeting using the process and evaluate it, deciding how relevant the idea is to them in their situations.

Starting point

Ask students to work in pairs. Ask them to go through the stages for the prompts. What would they do first? What would the next step be? Ask students to work with another one or two pairs and compare their stages. Ask them to work out which stages are essential and which are useful, but perhaps not essential. Provide whole-class feedback by asking two or three groups to report their ideas to the class.

Possible answers

Applying for a job: see advert, fill in application form, contact references, send in form, receive letter, go to interview, write an email of thanks for the interview, wait for reply.

Moving your office: find new location, contact moving company, buy packing boxes, throw away some items, pack other items, move in, choose desk location, unpack boxes.

Buying a house: visit estate agent / look online, visit houses, apply for mortgage, make offer, negotiate price, agree contract, agree day to exchange contracts.

Working with words

Exercise 1

Allow students a few minutes to think about the questions and then ask them to discuss their ideas with a partner.

Possible answers

Buying recycled paper for the printers, using the back of printed paper for notes, etc., making sure printer is set to print both sides, only printing in colour when necessary.

Making sure printer inks and toner are properly recycled (they contain chemicals that need proper storage).

Separate bins for bottles, paper, food, etc. in staff kitchens.

PRE-WORK LEARNERS Ask students to think about their college; what happens to waste paper, old books, out-of-date equipment, what happens to food waste, plastic bottles, etc.? Is it easy to recycle or do they have to look for recycling bins? Is there a clear and well-expressed policy that all students and staff are aware of?

Exercise 2

▶ 14.1 Ask students to look at the company profile and decide what sort of information they are listening for. Play the listening and ask them to complete the information. They can then discuss the answers with a partner. Provide feedback on answers with the whole class. If necessary, play the listening again, pausing to elicit the correct answers.

Answers
1 2002
2 21
3 $20 million
4 anything that is thrown away such as cigarette stubs, coffee capsules or biscuit wrappers
5 products like bags, benches and dustbins
6 Kenco
7 make a donation to the company's favourite charity

Exercise 3

Ask students to discuss the questions in small groups. Ask them if they think this kind of company is a good thing. Why/Why not? Provide whole-class feedback by asking each group to report their ideas back to the whole class.

Exercise 4

▶ 14.1 Tell students to read the sentences and then replace the words in bold with a multi-word verb from the list. Remind them to make sure the form of the verb is correct. You may want to do the first one as a model.

Answers	
1 cut down on	6 pick out, make
2 turning (it) into	(something new) out of
3 set up	7 take away
4 pick up	8 drop off
5 throw away	9 sign up

DICTIONARY SKILLS

Put students into three groups, A, B, C. Give each group a list of multi-word verbs, Group A: *get away, wear away, give away, put away, run away*; Group B: *drive off; switch off, put off, go off, log off*; Group C: *look up, give up, end up, show up, fill up*. Ask students in each group to check the meaning of each of their group's multi-word verbs in their dictionaries. When they have checked the meaning, they should then make a sentence with an option for the students in the other group to choose the correct one. For example, *take away: Every Tuesday the council takes away / throws away the recycling from the factory.*

Now regroup the students with one or two As, Bs, Cs in each group. Each student or pair teaches the others in the new group their multi-word verbs, giving their definitions and then reading their sentence for the others to choose the correct option. Monitor, checking the students' definitions and sentences.

Exercise 5

Students work in pairs. Explain that they are going to describe the process where individuals recycle items with TerraCycle, using some of the multi-word verbs in **4**. Refer students to the *Tip*. Tell students to follow the process as illustrated in the flow chart.

Then provide whole-class feedback, making sure students are using the correct verb forms.

Possible answers
1 Local businesses have to <u>sign up</u> to become a drop-off point.
2 TerraCycle don't <u>pick up</u> waste from individual homes, so the customer will have to <u>drop it off</u> at the special TerraCycle drop-off point.
3 The customer can <u>throw their rubbish away</u> there.
4 The TerraCycle truck will <u>pick up</u> the waste from the drop-off point and it will then go to the Recycling site.
5 There TerraCycle will <u>turn</u> the things people <u>throw away into</u> something useful.
6 Even items like cigarette stubs and coffee capsules can be <u>turned into</u> a new and useful item.

Further practice

If students need more practice, go to *Practice file 14* on page 132 of the *Student's Book*.

Exercise 6

Tell students to work in pairs and answer the questions. Check answers in whole-class feedback.

PRE-WORK LEARNERS   Ask students to discuss these questions with a partner or in small groups.

1 What sort of things do you throw away most days?
2 Do you think about recycling when you throw things away? If not, why not? Is it hard to find places to recycle?
3 What could you do to recycle more?
4 What sort of things does your college throw away every day? What could your college do to recycle more?
5 Is it possible to set up points around your college, or in your town, for certain types of rubbish to be recycled? Would you use them? Why/Why not?

Ask students to report back on the main points each pair or group made.

Exercise 7

Regroup the students so they work with another pair. Tell students to imagine this team has to improve recycling around the company. Ask them to discuss different ways to do this and to come up with a list of four or five action points.

ONE-TO-ONE   Ask the student to think of at least five ways his/her company might improve recycling. If the company already has a good recycling policy, ask him/her to explain what happens.

PRE-WORK LEARNERS   Tell students to imagine their team has to improve recycling around the local area, including their college. Ask them to discuss different ways to do this and to come up with a list of four or five action points.

Exercise 8

Each group presents its action plan in **7** to the class. The listeners should ask questions to get more details and decide if the ideas are achievable or not.

You could then ask the class to come up with a class list of the best five ideas from all of the groups.

Photocopiable worksheet

Download and photocopy *Unit 14 Working with words worksheet* from the teacher resources in the *Online practice*.

Language at work

Exercise 1

Ask students to work in pairs and follow the instructions. Ask one or two pairs to give feedback to the whole class. Don't give the students all the information at this time, as they will find it out in the following exercises.

Possible answers
Fuel and energy: fossil fuels – coal or gas, electricity, petrol, diesel, biofuels, fats, oil, air turbines, waves, hydro-power, hydrogen, helium, horsepower, nuclear power, solar, geothermal, steam, fire, etc.
Liquids: some gases, some fossil fuels
For cars: electricity, petrol, diesel, hydrogen
Renewables: waves, air, biofuels, solar
Under the ground: coal, gas, uranium, geothermal

Exercise 2

Tell students they are going to read an article about the uses of cooking oils and fat. Ask them to try to think of at least two different uses for these before they read it. Tell them to look at the picture, read the article and answer the questions. Let them compare answers with a partner. Check the answers in whole-class feedback. Were their original uses mentioned in the article?

Answer
The article describes cooking oil and fat used in heating, candles, soap and cosmetics and in biofuels.

Exercise 3

Ask students to read sentences 1–6 which have active form verbs in bold. Tell them to find the same information in the text in **2** in passive form. Let them check their answers with a partner. Check answers in whole-class feedback.

Answers
2	is used	5	to be reprocessed
3	can be turned into	6	are being driven
4	has been collected		

Exercise 4

Tell students to read the sentences in **3** and match the passive form of the verbs to the tenses and forms. They then find more passive verbs in the text and match them to the tenses and forms. Students compare answers with a partner and then do whole-class feedback.

Answers
Present simple 2 (is used, is given, is taken)
Past simple 1 (was turned, were made, were cooked in)
Present continuous 6 (are being driven)
Present perfect 4 (has been collected)
Infinitive 5 (to be reprocessed)
Modal 3 (can be turned into)

Exercise 5

Students work in pairs. Ask them to read the sentences in the *Language point* and then to complete the information by writing *passive* or *active* for 2–4. Provide whole-class feedback, eliciting why each answer is correct.

Answers
2 active
3 passive
4 passive

Grammar reference
If students need more information, go to *Grammar reference* on page 133 of the *Student's Book*.

Exercise 6

Ask students to read the text and underline the correct verb forms. Let them check their answers with a partner. Provide whole-class feedback, eliciting why the answers are correct.

Answers
2	have tried	6	was originally used
3	is needed	7	to be processed
4	can be grown	8	is being carried out
5	contain	9	will be used

EXTENSION Put students into three groups. Ask each group to research one form of renewable energy on the Internet, for example, solar energy, hydroelectricity or geothermal energy. Each group then prepares a presentation on their chosen form of energy. Then ask each group to present its information to the class. Finally, they can decide as a class which form of renewable energy is the most efficient and would be the most suitable for their region.

Further practice
If students need more practice, go to *Practice file 14* on page 133 of the *Student's Book*.

Exercise 7

Ask students to work in pairs. Give them time to think of the answers for their company and how to express these using the passive form. The students take turns to tell their partner about their company. Monitor, checking they are using the correct passive forms.

PRE-WORK LEARNERS Ask students to work in small groups. Tell them to think of a famous company and, if possible, look on the Internet to find out the information needed to complete the sentences.

Photocopiable worksheet
Download and photocopy *Unit 14 Language at work worksheet* from the teacher resources in the *Online practice*.

Practically speaking

Exercise 1

Ask students to work in pairs. Tell them to look at the pictures A–F and decide which part of the process each picture shows. Provide whole-class feedback, eliciting the correct answers.

Exercise 2

▶ 14.2 Tell students to listen and check their ideas. Play the listening. Check the answers in whole-class feedback. If necessary, play the listening again, pausing to elicit the correct answers.

Exercise 3

▶ 14.2 Tell students to read the expressions and then listen and number them in the order they hear them. Play the listening again. Check answers in whole-class feedback.

Answers
1 Let me explain how we …
4 First of all ,…
3 Essentially, there are … main stages.
5 After the … have been …, they are …
6 Having taken …, you …
2 The basic process is …
7 What you end up with is …
8 It's also worth noting that …

Exercise 4

Ask students to work in pairs and take turns to explain the jatropha process using the pictures in **1** and the expressions in **3**. Then ask students to check their answers in the audio script on page 157.

Exercise 5

Students work in pairs. Give them time to choose a process and prepare how to explain it to their partner. Ask them to take turns to explain the process they have chosen. The partner can ask questions to clarify anything they don't quite understand. Ask them to evaluate the processes and think of ways they could be improved. Monitor, checking that students are explaining clearly and using the appropriate expressions.

PRE-WORK LEARNERS Ask students to think of processes at their college, for example, how to apply for a course, how to organize an event at college. Ask them to explain the processes, then evaluate them and think of ways they could be improved.

Business communication

Exercise 1

Ask students to discuss the questions with a partner. Check answers in whole-class feedback by asking two or three students to report back.

PRE-WORK LEARNERS Ask students to discuss the questions in relation to their college. If they don't know the answers, tell them how to find out. Then ask them to find out and report back to the class in the next lesson.

Exercise 2

▶ 14.3 Explain to students that they are going to listen to three separate parts of a presentation about a new procedure for reporting injuries at work. Tell them to answer the questions as they listen. Play the listening. Let the students check their answers with a partner, then check the answers in whole-class feedback. If necessary, play the listening again, pausing to elicit the correct answers.

Answers
1 Within 24 hours
2 The team leader or the co-team leader
3 Any type (serious or less serious)

Exercise 3

▶ 14.3 Before students listen, ask them to read the expressions from the presentation. Then play the listening again for students to tick the expressions they hear. Check the answers in whole-class feedback. If necessary, play the listening again, pausing to elicit the correct answers.

Answers
If anyone has any questions, I'm happy to try and answer them now.
That's a good question.
I think there are two parts to that question.
First of all … And for your second point …
Sorry, I don't quite understand the question.
Let me check I've understood you correctly.
You're asking me if …?
Does that answer your question?

| **Further practice**
If students need more practice, go to *Practice file 14* on page 132 of the *Student's Book*.

Exercise 4

Students work in pairs. Ask them to discuss the five situations and decide how they would respond in each. What would be the best expression to use? Monitor, checking they are using the correct expressions. Provide whole-class feedback by asking two or three pairs to give their suggestions. You could ask the class if they think these are the best expressions to use in each situation.

Possible answers
1 Sorry, I couldn't hear you. Can you repeat that?
2 Let me check I've understood you correctly. You're asking me if …?
3 That's an important question.
4 Have I answered your question?
5 I think there are two parts to your question. I'll answer your first point and then deal with your second. First of all …

Exercise 5

Ask each student to choose a topic to give a 60-second presentation on. They should structure the presentation correctly, using suitable expressions to introduce the topic, and describe either their company and its products, or the structure they used in **5** on page 95 or a hobby or interest they have outside of work. At the end of the presentation, they will be asked questions. Refer students to the *Key expressions* to help them invite questions, check understanding, structure their answers and check they have answered the question satisfactorily.

Exercise 6

Tell students to work in small groups. They take turns to give their presentations. Everyone listening to each presentation should try to think of two or three questions to ask the speaker. At the end of the exercise each student can decide if he/she covered:

- inviting questions
- checking understanding
- commenting on the question
- structuring the answer
- checking he/she has answered the question satisfactorily.

The speaker could ask the others in the group to tell him/her one thing he/she did well and one area he/she needs to work on.

ONE-TO-ONE Ask the student to prepare a presentation on at least one of the topics in **5**. While he/she is giving his/her presentation, write at least two questions for him/her to answer. To give the student practice in listening and asking questions, you could prepare a 60-second presentation of your own and let him/her ask you two or three questions.

| **Photocopiable worksheet**
Download and photocopy *Unit 14 Business communication worksheet* from the teacher resources in the *Online practice*.

Talking point

Discussion

Exercise 1

Ask students to answer the questions in small groups. What makes meetings efficient or inefficient? Ask them to come up with three suggestions for making meetings more efficient. Ask one or two students to give feedback to the whole class.

> **Possible answers**
> Have time limits – no meeting to last longer than 30 minutes.
> Have a meeting where everyone stands.
> Have an agenda and stick to it.

PRE-WORK LEARNERS Ask students to discuss meetings they have at school or college, or in their personal life.

Exercise 2

Ask students if they have heard of Lean Management. You could give a couple of clues, and ask them what is normally lean or not (meat). Is it good if something is lean? Why/Why not? Then ask them to read the article and answer the questions with a partner. Check answers by asking one or two pairs for their ideas.

> **Possible answer**
> Everyone feels they have input into the meetings and can raise things that are important to them.

Exercise 3

Ask students to discuss the questions with a partner. Check answers by asking one or two pairs for their ideas.

PRE-WORK LEARNERS Ask students to discuss the idea of Lean Coffee meetings. Do they think they would be useful? Can they think of a situation where they could use this format? Would they be happy to take part in meetings like these? Ask them to think of up to three advantages, and up to three disadvantages, of having meetings like this.

Task

Exercise 1

Students work in groups of four or five and hold a Lean Coffee meeting. Tell students to follow the instructions.

ONE-TO-ONE Ask the student to think about how a Lean Coffee meeting on the topic would be useful. How different would it be from his/her company? Ask him/her to list advantages and disadvantages of this style of meeting. Ask him/her if he/she thinks this type of meeting would work in their company structure and to give reasons for their answer.

PRE-WORK LEARNERS Ask students to hold a Lean Coffee meeting to discuss things they would like to improve in their school or college.

Exercise 2

Each group evaluates the meeting style. Did they find the process easy to follow? What, if anything, created problems or caused delays? Did they think it was an effective way of running a meeting? Why/Why not? Can they think of ways to adapt the process to make it suit their workplace?

Provide whole-class feedback, asking students to decide what they think of the process and give reasons for their answers.

Progress test

Download and photocopy *Unit 14 Progress test* and *Speaking test* from the teacher resources in the *Online practice.*

15 Performance

Context

The topic of *Performance* gives students the language to talk about and describe the performance review procedure at their workplace. Anybody who works, or plans to work, in business knows that it is essential for companies to review performance at regular intervals to assess how the company and the staff are performing. This procedure should have a positive outcome. To do this, students cover the language needed to describe reviews and awards, and how they motivate and encourage staff to improve performance.

Carrying out reviews is a situation where it is essential to describe accurately how someone has made progress or not. To do this, students will practise past tenses, in particular the past continuous and past perfect tenses to talk about stages and times. Students will also learn how to make generalizations and to be specific where needed.

In this unit, students will also learn the language necessary to carry out performance appraisals and set objectives. They will listen to an appraisal and role-play the process themselves. They will then set out a plan of action for performance improvement.

In the *Talking point*, students will read research on personality traits, specifically what makes an extrovert, an introvert or an ambivert. They will have the opportunity to discuss the merits of personality tests and methods to measure and assess people's behaviour and personality. They will then design their own personality test and work with a partner to test it. Finally, they will present their ideas and compare suggestions.

Starting point

Ask students to work in pairs and discuss the questions. Ask them to think about appraisals at work – Who does them? How do they approach them? How much input do they have in the process? Ask students to look at areas other than work and discuss how easy or difficult it is to assess performance, for example, sport – easy; parenting – difficult. Ask them to try to think of other areas where people measure success. Provide whole-class feedback by asking two or three pairs to report their ideas to the class.

Working with words

Exercise 1

Allow students a few minutes to think about the question and then ask them to discuss their ideas with a partner. Provide whole-class feedback by asking two or three pairs to describe the qualities they chose. You could find out which qualities were listed most often.

Exercise 2

Ask students to read the part of a newsletter and answer the questions. Tell students it's not necessary to understand all the words at this stage, only the general sense. They can then discuss the answers with a partner. Provide feedback on answers with the whole class.

> **Answers**
> 1 Howard Lawrence feels the scheme is a success but is not surprised.
> 2 Staff and patients can recommend or nominate employees for the award.

Exercise 3

Ask students to discuss the questions in small groups. Ask them if they think employee reward schemes are a good thing. Why/Why not? Provide whole-class feedback by asking each group to report their ideas back to the whole class.

PRE-WORK LEARNERS Ask students how their performance is assessed at the moment. Is it only by exams, or do they have tutorials with their lecturers? Ask them which is better at motivating them to improve their performance. Ask them to give reasons.

Exercise 4

Tell students to work in pairs. Ask them to look at the words in bold in the article in **2** and identify which are adjectives and which are nouns. You could ask them how they decided that the words were nouns or adjectives, for example, the words around them, what form they have.

> **Answers**
> Adjectives: motivated, hard-working, dependable, efficient, caring
> Nouns: dedication, confidence, flexibility, enthusiasm, patience

Exercise 5

Students work in pairs. Ask them to read the nominations and then match one of the adjectives in **2** to the descriptions of the people nominated. Then provide whole-class feedback on the answers.

Answers
1	hard-working	4	caring
2	motivated	5	dependable
3	efficient		

EXTENSION Ask students to think of opposites to the adjectives in **5**.

Possible answers
hard-working	lazy, idle
motivated	unmotivated, demotivated
efficient	inefficient, incompetent
caring	uncaring, indifferent
dependable	undependable, unreliable

Ask students to write five sentences describing people who are one of the positive or negative adjectives (without using the adjectives themselves). They then take turns to read the sentences to a partner, who has to decide which adjective the description matches. Monitor, checking the sentences are clear.

Exercise 6

Tell students to work in pairs. They think of a colleague to nominate for employee of the month and describe them using the adjectives in **5**. Check answers in whole-class feedback by asking two or three students to describe their colleague.

PRE-WORK LEARNERS Ask students to think of a friend or classmate and describe him/her using the adjectives from **5**. Check answers in whole-class feedback by asking two or three students to describe their friend or classmate.

Exercise 7

Ask students to look at the newsletter in **2** again quickly and match the nouns in bold to the endings.

Answers
confidence, dedication, enthusiasm, flexibility

Exercise 8

Tell students to work in pairs. Ask them to complete the table with an adjective or noun form. Check answers in whole-class feedback.

Answers
1	dedication	6	enthusiasm
2	motivated	7	punctuality
3	flexibility	8	creative
4	confidence	9	ambition
5	efficient		

DICTIONARY SKILLS
Draw the stress patterns (see Answers below) on the board. Ask students to work in pairs and check their dictionaries to find the stress in the nouns in **8**. Check the answers with the whole class and then ask students to spend a few minutes practising the words.

Answers
Oo patience	**oOoo** efficiency
Ooo confidence	**ooOo** dedication, motivation
oOo ambition	**ooOoo** flexibility, creativity

Exercise 9

Tell students to complete the sentences with the correct form of a word from **8**. Let them compare answers with a partner. Then they take turns to say to a partner if the sentences are true or false for them, using a different form of the word. Check answers in whole-class feedback.

Answers
2 patient, e.g. *I don't have a lot of patience …*
3 punctuality, e.g. *I'm always punctual …*
4 confidence, e.g. *I have a lot of confidence in …*
5 motivation, e.g. *My company offers good incentives to keep its staff enthusiastic and motivated.*
6 dedicated, e.g. *I think dedication is important …*

PRE-WORK LEARNERS You could replace the following sentence for students to say if they are true or false:

4 I have a great deal of _____ in my teachers.
5 My school or college offers incentives to ensure ongoing enthusiasm and _____ amongst the students.
6 The teachers are _____ to the students and put their needs first.

Further practice

If students need more practice, go to *Practice file 15* on page 134 of the *Student's Book*.

Exercise 10

Ask students to think of three job titles and to write down the qualities they think someone would need for the job. You could ask them to discuss their ideas in small groups and come up with a group list.

Provide whole-class feedback by asking each student or each group to list the qualities needed, and ask them to give reasons for their choices. The class decides if they agree.

Exercise 11

Students work in pairs and talk about the qualities that are important for their job. Tell students to describe themselves and how their qualities help them do their job.

Provide whole-class feedback by asking three or four pairs to report back to the class.

PRE-WORK LEARNERS Ask students to think of their ideal job. Ask them to work in pairs and talk about what qualities are important for the job they chose. Ask them to describe themselves, decide if they have those qualities and say how these qualities would help them do their ideal job.

Photocopiable worksheet

Download and photocopy *Unit 15 Working with words worksheet* from the teacher resources in the *Online practice*.

Language at work

Exercise 1

Ask students to discuss the questions with a partner. Ask one or two pairs to give feedback to the whole class.

PRE-WORK LEARNERS Ask students how they feel when getting feedback on their work. Ask them what kind of feedback they find the most helpful.

Exercise 2

▶ 15.1 Tell students they are going to listen to Ahmed talking about his new job. Ask them to look at the questions to know what they are listening for. Play the listening. Let them compare answers with a partner. Check the answers in whole-class feedback. If necessary, play the listening again, pausing to elicit the correct answers.

Answers
1 Because he was having problems with his previous company. Also, he didn't like the town.
2 Because he was living in a new city.
3 Because the feedback in his first performance review was positive.

Exercise 3

▶ 15.1 Ask students to read sentences 1–3 and choose the option they think is correct. Let them check their answers with a partner. Play the listening again to check the answers. Check answers in whole-class feedback.

Answers
1 was having
2 had opened
3 was living

Exercise 4

Tell students to read the sentences in **3** again and complete the information in the *Language point*. Students compare answers with a partner and then do whole-class feedback.

You could ask the students to turn to the audio script on page 157 and underline the past perfect and past continuous tenses.

Answers
2, 3, 1

Grammar reference

If students need more information, go to *Grammar reference* on page 135 of the *Student's Book*.

Exercise 5

▶ 15.2 Ask students to read the questions. Play the listening. Let students check their answers with a partner. Check answers in whole-class feedback.

Answers
1 Helena: She was told that if she didn't work as part of a team, she'd never get anywhere in the company.
  Matthias: His manager said he was doing really well, but the review said he would only get a three per cent raise.
2 Helena: Six months later, she was transferred to another subsidiary and six months after that, she was running the factory.
  Matthias: Some weeks later, he heard that his manager was fired, but he'd already left by then.

Exercise 6

▶ 15.2 Ask students to read the sentences from the listening and complete them with a past perfect or past continuous form. Let them check their answers with a partner. Play the listening again. Provide whole-class feedback by playing the listening again, eliciting why the answers are correct.

Answers
1 was working
2 had/'d already discussed
3 was running
4 were talking
5 had prepared
6 had/'d already left

In sentence 6, the emphasis or contrast is on the two events: 1) hearing news about something and not on the news itself (that he got fired), and 2) that this happened after the person who was speaking had already left the job.

Further practice

If students need more practice, go to *Practice file 15* on page 135 of the *Student's Book*.

Exercise 7

Ask students to look at the timeline. Make sure that they understand the difference between *periods* and *events*. You could ask them which lasts longer and which happens once, or regularly. Ask students to work in pairs and make sentences about Helena, using past perfect and past continuous forms.

Possible answers
Helena had a bad performance appraisal while she was working for a food company. She transferred to another company because she had/'d had a bad performance review.
While she was working for a subsidiary company, she was asked to run the subsidiary, even though she had/'d had a bad performance review while she was working for her previous company.

Exercise 8

Ask students to make a timeline about their past. They can use Helena's in **7** as a model. Make sure they are only talking about their past, not their present situation. Ask them to put the periods of time and the important events on the timeline. They can include any important events; about their studies, their career, or life events in general.

You might want to model this exercise by putting your own timeline on the board and covering the areas suggested. Students could then make sentences about you for extra practice.

Ask students to work in pairs and describe their timeline with its periods of time and events. Provide whole-class feedback by asking students to report back on their partner's timeline.

Photocopiable worksheet

Download and photocopy *Unit 15 Language at work worksheet* from the teacher resources in the *Online practice*.

Practically speaking

Exercise 1

Ask students to work in pairs. Tell them to discuss the last time they had an interview. Ask one or two pairs to report back to the whole class on their experiences.

PRE-WORK LEARNERS Ask students to work in small groups. Ask them to imagine they are going to a job interview. Ask the groups to write six to eight questions they think they could be asked. Then they should decide what the best answers would be. Regroup the students and ask them to report back on their questions and answers.

Exercise 2

▶ **15.3** Tell students to listen to part of a job interview and answer the questions. Tell them to read the questions before they listen. Play the listening. Let them check their answers with a partner. Check the answers in whole-class feedback. If necessary, play the listening again, pausing to elicit the correct answers.

> **Answers**
> 1 What's one thing about your job that you've found challenging and how have you dealt with it?
> 2 That they were all quite different characters so it was hard to get everyone to work together. One of the team was very independent.
> 3 That it was a success and that he learnt a lot from it.

Exercise 3

Tell students to read the expressions in bold in the two sentences and decide which is generalizing and which is specifying. Check answers in whole-class feedback.

> **Answers**
> Generalizing 2
> Specifying 1

Exercise 4

Ask students to work in pairs and decide which of the words have a similar meaning to the words in bold in **3**. Some expressions are generalizing and some are specifying. Check answers in whole-class feedback.

> **Answers**
> overall (generalizing): generally, all in all, mainly, mostly, in general, generally speaking
> in particular (specifying): particularly, especially, specifically

Exercise 5

Students work in pairs. Refer students to the *Tip*. Tell them to read sentences 1–5 and then make them general or specific. Check answers in whole-class feedback, paying particular attention to the word order.

> **Possible answers**
> 2 Generally speaking, my company does more and more business online these days.
> 3 We mostly communicate in English at work.
> 4 My last holiday was especially relaxing.
> 5 All in all, I'm happy with my job at the moment. / I'm particularly happy with my job at the moment.

Exercise 6

Give students a short time to prepare their answers to the three questions. They then work in pairs and take turns to ask and answer the questions. They should give as much detail as possible, remembering to use expressions to generalize and to specify. Provide whole-class feedback by asking three or four pairs to role-play the interview in front of the class. After the feedback, ask the students which question/ questions they found particularly difficult to answer. Ask them to give reasons for their answers.

Business communication

Exercise 1

Ask students to read the appraisal form. Ask them if they have ever filled in a form like this and how they felt / would feel doing it. Check answers in whole-class feedback by asking two or three students about their responses.

PRE-WORK LEARNERS Ask students if they ever have reviews in college and, if so, what is reviewed. Ask them if they think the questions are relevant to them, and, if they aren't, how they could change them to make them more relevant.

Exercise 2

▶ **15.4** Tell students they are going to listen to the first part of Chris's performance review and that they should add in any extra information they hear. Play the listening. Let the students check their answers with a partner. Check the answers in whole-class feedback. If necessary, play the listening again, pausing to elicit the correct answers.

> **Possible answers**
> 3 This interests me and I'd like to develop this area.
> 4 Perhaps work on my abilities to work with others and my teamwork skills.

Exercise 3

▶ **15.4** Students work in pairs. Ask them to read the expressions from the review and match 1–7 to a–g, then play the listening again for students to check. Check the answers in whole-class feedback. If necessary, play the listening again, pausing to elicit the correct answers.

> **Answers**
> 1 c 2 f 3 a 4 g 5 e 6 d 7 b

Exercise 4

▶ **15.5** Tell students to listen to the final part of Chris's performance review and answer the questions. Play the listening. Let students check their answers with a partner, then check the answers in whole-class feedback. If necessary, play the listening again, pausing to elicit the correct answers.

Further practice

If students need more practice, go to *Practice file 15* on page 134 of the *Student's Book*.

Exercise 5

Ask students to imagine they have a performance review. Tell them to turn to page 141 and complete the form. You could photocopy the form for students to fill in. Monitor, checking they are filling it in correctly.

PRE-WORK LEARNERS Ask students to use the questions they wrote in **1** as their form and fill it in.

Exercise 6

Tell students to work in pairs. They take turns to appraise their partner using the form the partner has filled in. Refer them to the *Key expressions*. Tell students to follow the instructions to hold the meeting. It is important that there is a level of formality or structure to the meeting, as it is an important stage in everyone's career.

Exercise 7

Students work in pairs. Give them a few minutes to choose a topic and decide what improvements they could make. They take turns to review their partner's performance and decide on a plan of action to make improvements. Provide whole-class feedback by asking three or four pairs to report back on their plans of action, giving reasons why they chose the actions they did.

Photocopiable worksheet

Download and photocopy *Unit 15 Business communication worksheet* from the teacher resources in the *Online practice*.

Talking point

Discussion

Exercise 1

Ask students to read the article and discuss the answer to the question with a partner.

PRE-WORK LEARNERS Ask students to answer the question in relation to their ideal job.

Exercise 2

Ask students to discuss the questions with a partner. Ask students to give their reactions to this sort of research. Check answers by asking one or two pairs for their ideas. Do they think it is useful, or fake/pseudo-science? Ask students for their reasons for their answers.

Exercise 3

Ask students if they have ever done a personality test. Did it tell them anything interesting about themselves? Did they trust what it said? Why/Why not?

Task

Exercise 1

Ask students how they feel about the example sentence. Is it true for them? How would they score themselves?

Exercise 2

Students work in pairs and design a personality test. They write five more sentences to find out if someone is extrovert, introvert or ambivert.

Exercise 3

Students swap their test with another pair's and both pairs do the test and score it.

They then compare both pairs' tests to see if they think they are accurate. Ask them to give reasons for their evaluation.

Progress test

Download and photocopy *Unit 15 Progress test* and *Speaking test* from the teacher resources in the *Online practice*.

Viewpoint 5

Exercise 1

▶ 01 Ask students to read the questions in the table to see what they are watching for. Play the video and ask students to take notes. If necessary, pause after each speaker to allow writing time. Let students check their answers with a partner. Check answers in whole-class feedback.

Answers

1
Speaker 1
Yes: Has a 'Green Impact' initiative and sustainability policy; departments monitor recycling and use of resources; students and staff think of ways to improve recycling and ways to help the environment
Speaker 2
Yes: Strives to reduce its 'carbon footprint'; recycling of and restricting use of water; recycle cardboard; food bank for unused food
Speaker 3
Yes: Recently named one of top green companies in the US; related to design of offices and not using much paper (through e-commerce)
2
Speaker 2
A company comes and checks for Legionnaires' (Disease) in standing water; takes water samples and water temperatures; strict code to keep students safe
3
Speaker 3
Will put on the career page and media section of website; [because] everyone sensitive to how we use environment, especially younger people; important factor for potential employees

Exercise 2

Ask students to work in pairs and take turns to ask and answer the three questions in the table/video about their own company.

PRE-WORK LEARNERS Ask students to list the main environmental issues in their local area, in order of seriousness.

Exercise 3

Tell students they are going to watch a video and that all of these words come up in it. Ask them to match the words

1–10 to the definitions a–j. Let students check their answers with a partner. Check answers in whole-class feedback.

Answers
2 c 3 h 4 i 5 e 6 f 7 d 8 j 9 g 10 b

Exercise 4

▶ 02 Ask students to read the headings A–F and as they watch the video put them in the correct order 1–6. Play the video. Let students check their answers with a partner. Check answers in whole-class feedback.

Answers
A 2 B 4 C 1 D 5 E 3 F 6

VIDEO SCRIPT

1 What does your company do?
I work for a company called Hillbreak and we offer environmental sustainability services to a range of different organizations.

2 What are the main reasons why a company would use your services?
There are two principle reasons, or drivers as we call them, which would encourage a different organization to come to us for different types of services. The first one relates to the law, to regulations which come as a result of legislation. There is a lot of environmental legislation and thus regulation in the European Union, although all member states have their different ways of implementing the regulations. Different businesses, whether they are private sector businesses or public sector organizations – and we work for both of those different categories – will come to us because they know that they have to comply with certain types of regulation, or that they have a suspicion that there may be environmental regulations that they should be complying with that they don't know about.

3 What's the other reason why a business uses your service?
The second type of driver that leads organizations to come to us for services relates very much to market drivers. So putting the regulations to one side, an organization, a business or a city council for example, might come to us and say, what can we do, what should we be doing, in order to improve what we have to offer to the market place? So for example, a building owner would come to us and say, we know we have to comply with the regulations but what else can we do to make our building have more appeal to the market place so that tenants may come to our office building for example, because they know that they want to occupy premises which have what you might call "green appeal", or good environmental practice.

4 What's an example of a building with 'green appeal'?
You can think of many examples where this is the case. For example, take an iconic building in central London, like the Shard. There is a building, which when it was constructed, would have had to comply with a lot of environmental regulations, called building regulations and building codes. It would also, because the owners wanted to make sure that the building had as wide appeal as possible to potential occupiers, they wanted to go above and beyond that environmental regulation to make sure that they had green certificates which demonstrated that the building was environmentally responsible in the way that it was built.

5 What is an example of a business which has benefitted from your consultancy's help?
There are lots of those, but one which I think might be particularly useful to think about is in the context of retail stores. So we have a client who is a global retailer of sportswear who came to us and said, we want to have a program of refurbishing all of our stores to give them a fresh appeal to the market place. We want and we know we will have to comply with environmental regulations, building regulations, to ensure that the materials that we use are appropriate, but we want to go further than that to make sure that the way that we refurbish these buildings is environmentally responsible. So it was our job to help advise them about the sorts of materials and sorts of systems like heating and cooling that they might use in their stores were as environmentally responsible as possible. We worked on a number of case study pilots buildings in the UK and other parts of Western Europe to make sure that the building system that we were designing worked in a number of different jurisdictions. We then had some pilots in, pilot case studies in North and South America and one in China to make sure it worked again in those different jurisdictions. And now that retailer is able to roll out that system of improving the environmental performance of its buildings when it's refurbishing its stores right across the globe.

6 Why are urban development projects important for cities?
We work with a lot of organizations at the city council level both in the UK and in other jurisdictions. City councils have come to realize that the way that they plan their cities, the way that they design urban environments, is really important in terms of being able to provide a brand for their city. And you can find some really good examples of this. If you take New York City for example, and you think about some of the fantastic projects in terms of urban design that have been developed there - you can think of the Highline for example, which is a fantastic project and lots of other cities look to those sorts of examples and think how can we in our local cultural context how can we ensure that we improve the urban design of our particular urban spaces and bring those together to provide something which helps to develop the brand of particular cities, so we've come to work with lots of different city councils around the world to help them to identify what brand they're hoping to achieve and how urban design can really help them to ensure that that brand is propagated into the market place.

Exercise 5

▶ 02 Students work in pairs. Ask them to read the questions and answer as many as they can from memory. Play the video again for them to check and add to their answers. Check answers in whole-class feedback. If necessary, play the video again, pausing it for students to hear the answers.

Answers
1 Environmental sustainability services to a range of different organizations.
2 The first one relates to the law, to regulations which come as a result of legislation.
3 Private and public sectors use Hillbreak consultancy.
4 Market drivers.
5 Whether the building has 'green appeal' or not.
6 They wanted to make sure that the building had as wide appeal as possible to potential occupiers.
7 Sportswear.
8 To help advise on the sorts of materials and sorts of systems like heating and cooling that they might use in their stores to make sure they were as environmentally responsible as possible.
9 In the beginning in the UK and Western Europe, and later in North and South America, in China and now the retailer can refurbish all its shops globally.
10 By the way you design an urban environment.
11 The Highline in New York

Exercise 6

Students work in pairs. Ask them to use some of the words in **3** to complete the sentences. Check answers in whole-class feedback.

Answers

1 driver	4 refurbish
2 comply with	5 regulations
3 jurisdiction	6 urban design

Exercise 7

Ask students to answer the questions in small groups.

PRE-WORK LEARNERS Ask students if they think their college or university has 'green appeal', and what things could they do to brand it in this way.

Exercise 8

Students work in small groups and follow the instructions. Then the students present their ideas to their own group, and the group chooses the best idea or thinks of a new one.

Exercise 9

Each group gives its presentation. Students present their choice and give reasons for it. You could get the class to vote on which was the most convincing presentation and the best idea.

ONE-TO-ONE Ask the student to prepare a presentation for you, following the instructions in **8** and explaining his/her reasons for the choices.

Further video ideas

You can find a list of suggested ideas for how to use video in the class in the teacher resources in the *Online practice*.

Practice file answer key

Unit 1

Working with words

Exercise 1
2 a   3 e   4 h   5 g   6 c   7 f   8 d

Exercise 2
1 charge of
2 responsible for
3 consist of
4 specialize in
5 work with / deal with
6 deal with / work with

Business communication

Exercise 1
2 this is
3 I'm very pleased
4 Nice to meet you
5 what do you do
6 Really
7 It was nice
8 Here's my

Exercise 2
2 I'm delighted to meet you
3 Please call me Greg
4 Which part of the US are you from
5 I'm afraid I have to go now
6 It was very nice to meet you
7 Do you have a card
8 I look forward to hearing from you

Language at work

Exercise 1
2 do you have to
3 is she sitting
4 are you working on
5 does Nadia think
6 Are you thinking
7 does a successful salesperson earn
8 are you doing
9 think, belongs
10 have/are having

Exercise 2
2 I'm currently working on plans for a new shopping centre.
3 I often have lunch with clients.
4 She normally leaves at 4.00 on Friday afternoons.
5 All our customers expect free Wi-fi nowadays.
6 I never take work home at the weekend, even if we're really busy during the week.

Unit 2

Working with words

Exercise 1
2 core hours
3 overtime
4 home-working
5 statutory pay
6 lunch break
7 public holiday
8 paternity leave
9 unpaid leave
10 annual leave

Exercise 2
1 a   2 b   3 c   4 b   5 a   6 b

Business communication

Exercise 1
b Can you say that again
c Can I have his number
d Is that all lower case
e Was that GSA or GSI / Was that GSI or GSA
f Could you give me that

Exercise 2
1 a   2 c   3 f   4 b   5 e   6 d

Exercise 3
1 gec@hotmail.com
2 004431944010
3 lydia_49@yahoo.dt
4 www.about-me.com/courses_online

Language at work

Exercise 1
1 nice to see
2 difficult to know
3 important to be
4 afraid to leave
5 sad to see
6 right to ask

Exercise 2
1 to change
2 to join
3 being
4 applying
5 inviting
6 to take
7 developing
8 to help
9 to requalify
10 seeing

Exercise 3
1 arriving
2 to keep (to make)
3 offering
4 to make
5 interviewing
6 spending
7 to sum up
8 to talk

Unit 3

Working with words

Exercise 1
2 schedule
3 update
4 budget
5 deadline
6 teamwork
7 skills

Exercise 2
2 d   3 f   4 b   5 g   6 h   7 c   8 e

Exercise 3
1 deadline
2 schedule
3 allocated
4 resources
5 staff
6 budget
7 update

Business communication

Exercise 1
2 happening with
3 help with
4 where are
5 we're currently
6 anyone else
7 update me
8 So far
9 let's check
10 let's meet

Exercise 2
2 We've almost finished
3 is everything on track
4 is that something I can
5 and I'm going to

Language at work

Exercise 1
1 booked
2 Have
3 lived
4 haven't seen
5 changed
6 Did
7 hasn't arrived
8 I've asked

Exercise 2
2 closed
3 has just organized
4 Have you called
5 did she arrive
6 've / have ever met
7 didn't take
8 haven't improved
9 Have you ever spoken
10 have you worked

Exercise 3
1 yet   2 just   3 already

Unit 4

Working with words

Exercise 1
2 handy
3 accurate
4 secure
5 efficient
6 up-to-date
7 time-consuming
8 poor quality

Exercise 2
1 Hiring a consultant, helps
2 Having a financial advisor, allows
3 Online banking, makes
4 Flying business class, lets

Business communication

Exercise 1
1 problems
2 question
3 happens
4 convinced
5 allow
6 seem
7 find

Exercise 2

1 The main benefit is
2 It's also a lot less
3 Will it let
4 It'll let
5 make your life easier
6 That's probably true
7 makes things easier
8 another useful feature is

Language at work

Exercise 1

2 easy   6 slower
3 well   7 more original
4 friendlier   8 more popular
5 faster

Exercise 2

2 than   5 more   8 almost as
3 than   6 much   9 far
4 a bit   7 a bit

Unit 5

Working with words

Exercise 1

2 requirements   5 expectations
3 services   6 satisfaction
4 care

Exercise 2

1 caring   5 satisfied
2 expectations   6 delivery
3 require   7 productive
4 produce

Exercise 3

1 services   3 expect   5 care
2 loyalty   4 require   6 satisfy

Business communication

Exercise 1

2 fix   5 good   8 OK
3 arrange   6 suit   9 free
4 come   7 make   10 bring

Exercise 2

2 about   5 on   8 in
3 for   6 back
4 at   7 forward

Language at work

Exercise 1

2 gets in   7 are we doing
3 is meeting   8 're / are having
4 's / is bringing   9 does your flight
5 are we all having   leave
6 're / are showing   10 leaves

Exercise 2

2 Our team are going out to celebrate
Torsten's birthday.

---

3 We're / We are planning to meet in
reception around five.
4 I'm hoping (I hope) to try that new
Greek restaurant.
5 The last train leaves at midnight.
6 If you aren't / are not busy

Unit 6

Working with words

Exercise 1

2 exhibition   5 sightseeing
3 excursions   6 specialities
4 delegates   7 venue
(ALICANTE)

Exercise 2

2 check in   5 eat out
3 freshen up   6 look around
4 show you   7 pick you up
   around   8 meet up with

Business communication

Exercise 1

2 Did you have any trouble finding us
3 Don't worry about signing in
4 I'll run through today's programme
5 Come this way to my office
6 You'll need this badge to enter the
building
7 Make sure you sign in at reception

Exercise 2

2 how was your   5 I thought you
   journey   could
3 let me take your   6 catch up again
   bag   7 You'll need this
4 can I get you a   8 Make sure you
   drink

Language at work

Exercise 1

1 a   6 The   11 –
2 the   7 the   12 the
3 –   8 the   13 –
4 a   9 the   14 an
5 –   10 –

Exercise 2

2 Remember to wear an ID badge at all
times.
3 Check (the) visitors' names on the
registration list when they enter the
main venue.
4 If you see a visitor who looks lost,
immediately offer to help.
5 Staff not wearing a uniform will be sent
home.
6 The exhibition centre is always closed to
visitors on Mondays.
7 For information, direct (the) visitors to
the Central Registration Desk.
8 If you travel by car, please park in the
Staff Car Park.

Unit 7

Working with words

Exercise 1

2 network   5 encrypted
3 was down   6 prevent
4 hackers   7 vulnerable

Exercise 2

1 e   2 c   3 b   4 g   5 a   6 d   7 f

Business communication

Exercise 1

8 Is that any better?
3 Yes, Loud and clear. Hi, Natasha.
2 Yes, it is. Hello Ryan. Natasha is here with
me, too. Can you hear me OK?
1 Hello? Is that Michael?
7 Me neither. Ryan, your line isn't very
good. Can you speak up?
4 Hi, Ryan.
5 We're just waiting for Liza. She's calling
from Rome.
9 Yes, much better.
6 Sure. I haven't spoken to her for ages.
10 Hello? This is Liza.

Exercise 2

1 begin   5 question
2 discuss   6 covers
3 speak / start   7 sum
4 say   8 come

Language at work

Exercise 1

1 need to   5 mustn't
2 have to   6 can
3 doesn't have to   7 aren't allowed to
4 Can I / Am I   / mustn't
   allowed to   8 have to

Exercise 2

2 need to bring your laptop
3 allowed to smoke
4 can't / mustn't / aren't allowed to take
5 not allowed to talk
6 have to / must wear
7 allowed to use your password
8 have to drive on

Unit 8

Working with words

Exercise 1

Across:
2 capital   8 entrepreneurs
6 equity   9 forecasts
7 Shares
Down:
1 Commission   4 loan
3 investors   5 dividends

Exercise 2

1 for 2 back 3 towards 4 out

Business communication

Exercise 1

1 chart, divided into
2 upward
3 figures
4 continue

Exercise 2

1 at
2 on
3 into
4 from
5 to
6 in
7 over

Language at work

Exercise 1

2 am going to /'m going to
3 will /'ll
4 will /'ll
5 am going to /'m going to
6 will /'ll

Exercise 2

2 c 3 a 4 c 5 a 6 b

Unit 9

Working with words

Exercise 1

3 transportation
4 showrooms
5 inventory
6 middlemen
7 shipment
8 keep track
9 handmade
10 origin

Exercise 2

1 on
2 stock up on
3 out of
4 track of
5 low

Business communication

Exercise 1

2 Can I take your account details
3 look into it
4 according to my information
5 what has happened to it
6 you check it out for me
7 get back to you within the hour

Exercise 2

2 was dispatched on
3 must have gone wrong
4 check it out
5 asap
6 as quick as we can
7 charge it to

Language at work

Exercise 1

2 How much does it cost to send a magazine
3 Do you have any idea how long it takes

4 Would you mind telling me if a package has arrived
5 Has my visitor arrived yet
6 Could anyone tell me where the post office is
7 Do you know if they left a message for me
8 What day will my order arrive

Exercise 2

2 why you didn't call to say you'd be late
3 where the next conference is
4 which flight Mr Stoppard is on
5 if they are arriving tonight
6 how often the bus comes

Unit 10

Working with words

Exercise 1

2 futuristic
3 state-of-the-art
4 spacious
5 comfortable
6 fully-equipped
7 fun
8 old-fashioned

Exercise 2

1 isn't exactly
2 not very
3 really
4 pretty
5 fairly
6 very
7 extremely

Business communication

Exercise 1

2 change the colour
3 asking them to make a better offer
4 difficult to convince them of our proposals
5 we provide some chairs
6 having music in the factory
7 not come
8 you look at this again tomorrow morning

Exercise 2

2 good / great idea
3 will / would work
4 might prove
5 can / could always
6 Besides

Language at work

Exercise 1

2 ✓
3 ✓
4 ~~little~~ few
5 ~~many~~ much
6 ✓
7 ~~any~~ some
8 ~~fewer~~ less
9 ✓
10 ✓

Exercise 2

2 few
3 any / many
4 some / a lot
5 much
6 lot
7 any / many
8 any
9 few / lot of

Unit 11

Working with words

Exercise 1

2 e 3 a 4 b 5 f 6 d 7 g

Exercise 2

1 democratic
2 consultation
3 confrontation
4 hierarchical
5 cooperative

Exercise 3

2 consensus
3 member
4 evaluate
5 confrontation
6 decision

Business communication

Exercise 1

2 Do you have any concerns about this
3 I'll meet you halfway
4 I think that would be fair
5 If I offer 10% more, will you agree to two years
6 I'd like to discuss an issue with you
7 I'm not in a position to accept that

Exercise 2

2 issue
3 concern
4 problem
5 Supposing (Shall)
6 about
7 can

Language at work

Exercise 1

2 have, will end
3 work, 'll / will be
4 knew, 'd / would be
5 had, would they be
6 improves, 'll / will have to
7 would you feel, asked
8 would do, went
9 could, would you change
10 arrive, 'll / will be able to

Exercise 2

1 as soon as
2 When
3 Unless, will have
4 Unless, will look
5 will have to, if

Unit 12

Working with words

Exercise 1

2 dynamic
3 concept
4 reliable
5 simple
6 innovative
7 revolutionary
8 original
9 reinvention
10 sophisticated

Exercise 2

2 a 3 a 4 b 5 c 6 c 7 b 8 a

Business communication

Exercise 1

1	for	5	at	9	think
2	about	6	for	10	say
3	by	7	about		
4	at	8	to		

Exercise 2

1	Good	5	Then / Secondly
2	here	6	finally / lastly
3	start / begin	7	free
4	First / Firstly		

Exercise 3

2 d 3 k 4 a 5 e 6 g 7 b 8 l
9 i 10 f 11 c 12 j

Language at work

Exercise 1

2	the quickest	5	most bored
3	the most influential	6	the second most
4	beautiful places	7	you have ever
		8	the busiest

Exercise 2

2	worst	6	one
3	fewest	7	fewest
4	flexible	8	best
5	second		

Unit 13

Working with words

Exercise 1

1	failure	6	injury
2	refund	7	recalling
3	down	8	complaints
4	defect	9	mistake
5	damaged	10	resolved

Exercise 2

2 d 3 a 4 e 5 b 6 c

Business communication

Exercise 1

2	won't	6	Have you tried
3	do you mean by	7	think you should
4	keeps on	8	should solve the problem
5	sounds as though	9	if I were you

Exercise 2

2	's always borrowing	6	'd advise
3	taking	7	sounds
4	wrong	8	should
5	should	9	appears
		10	putting

Language at work

Exercise 1

2 e 3 a 4 c 5 b

Exercise 2

2 e, 4 c

Exercise 3

1	where	4	where
2	whose	5	when
3	who		

Exercise 4

2 They are the people whose company went bankrupt last year
3 Palo Alto is a city which has lots of tech businesses.
4 The lunchbreak is a time when you should relax.
5 Tennis is a sport which a lot employees play after work.

Unit 14

Working with words

Exercise 1

1	cut down (on)	6	drop off
2	throw away	7	pick out
3	turn into	8	pick up
4	take away	9	make out of
5	set up	10	sign up

Exercise 2

1	pick out	5	make, out of
2	throw away	6	drop off
3	set up	7	turn, into
4	cut down on	8	pick up

Business communication

Exercise 1

2 Does anyone have any questions?
3 I don't quite understand the question.
4 Let me check I've understood you correctly.
5 Thank you for that question.
6 That's an important question.
7 There are two parts to your question.
8 Does that answer your question?
9 Have I answered your question?

Exercise 2

2	questions, answer	5	check, correctly
3	hear, repeat	6	asking, if
4	quite, question	7	that, your

Language at work

Exercise 1

2	make	6	employs
3	are cut and painted	7	supports
4	sew	8	are encouraged and trained
5	are washed		

Exercise 2

2	is located	5	was won
3	was turned	6	has been used
4	was held		

Exercise 3

2 are being opened this year
3 must be given a warning if they are late
4 have agreed to extend the hours of work
5 is regarded as a sign of politeness in this culture

Unit 15

Working with words

Exercise 1

2	confident	5	hard-working
3	ambitious	6	enthusiastic
4	patient	7	punctual

Exercise 2

2	patience	6	flexible
3	confidence	7	enthusiasm
4	motivation	8	ambition
5	creativity		

Business communication

Exercise 1

2 pleased / happy
3 feel
4 happy / pleased
5 strengths
6 seem
7 thing / issue / problem

Exercise 2

2 about 3 for 4 with

Exercise 3

2	do	4	sound
3	intend	5	add

Language at work

Exercise 1

2	hadn't been	7	stopped
3	were all finishing	8	came across
4	said	9	hadn't liked
5	hadn't asked	10	had waited
6	was suggesting		

Exercise 2

2	had had	6	were running
3	were quickly becoming	7	had asked
4	was growing	8	hadn't you taken
5	had just graduated	9	was doing